Ko

By

JACK NEARY

Dramatic Publishing Company
Woodstock, Illinois ● Australia ● New Zealand ● South Africa

IMPORTANT BILLING AND CREDIT REQUIREMENTS

All producers of the play *must* give credit to the author of the play in all programs distributed in connection with performances of the play and in all instances in which the title of the play appears for purposes of advertising, publicizing or otherwise exploiting the play and/or a production. The name of the author *must* also appear on a separate line, on which no other name appears, immediately following the title, and *must* appear in size of type not less than fifty percent (50%) the size of the title type. Biographical information on the author, if included in the playbook, may be used in all programs. *In all programs this notice must appear:*

"Produced by special arrangement with
THE DRAMATIC PUBLISHING COMPANY, INC., of Woodstock, Illinois."

Abruptly, the main door opens. MYRON SIEGEL bursts inside and flips on the lights. MYRON is in his 40s, energized and driven. He is dressed to the nines—top hat, tails, the works. He flings his hat on the sofa as he assaults the telephone.)

MYRON *(entering)*. I knew it. I knew it. I knew it. I knew it. I knew it! *(Lifts receiver and slaps the bar energetically.)*

(SALLY CHARMAINE enters. She is MYRON's mother, blunt and brash. She appears to have started smoking in the womb. She, too, is dressed to the hilt.)

SALLY *(looking back out the door)*. He knew it! *(Goes directly to the bar and makes a drink.)*

MYRON. I knew it!

SALLY. I heard.

MYRON *(into the phone)*. Get me the Alhambra Theatre, please! … Backstage! *(To SALLY.)* I told you, I told Bertrille, I told anybody who'd listen to me. Carl Dennam was gonna sabotage my opening! I knew it!

(Meanwhile, DAISY has entered. She is a cute brunette in her 20s. She is bug-eyed and in general awe of everything, as if she just got off the bus from Buffalo. This is because she just got off the bus from Buffalo. She carries a dilapidated suitcase.)

DAISY *(surveys the room)*. Boy oh boy! This is big!

SALLY *(to DAISY)*. Didja hear? He knew it. *(Drinks.)*

DAISY. Like a liberry or somethin'!

SALLY. Daisy, take a load off. You've had a long trip.

DAISY. I never seen so many doors! Do they all really go someplace?

SALLY. Sit!

DAISY. I can't sit! Once I got off that bus, I told myself I'd never sit again!

MYRON *(into phone)*. Hello! I wanna talk to Carl Dennam!

DAISY. You could have a funeral in here!

MYRON *(into phone)*. Never mind who this is!

DAISY. You know, for like the Pope … or Hoot Gibson! *(Continues to check out the room.)*

MYRON. Carl Dennam!

SALLY *(aimed at MYRON)*. Twenty-one thousand, six hundred thirty-seven dollars …

MYRON. Shut up, Ma!

SALLY. And forty-two cents.

MYRON *(into phone)*. What? … Whatdya mean he's indisposed? … What? … Of course I know what indisposed means! *(Covers phone, to SALLY.)* What does "indisposed" mean?

SALLY. I left my dictionary at the Stork Club.

DAISY *(points at SALLY)*. Ha! Good one, Grandma!

SALLY *(to DAISY)*. Don't call me Grandma! *(To MYRON.)* My life savings. Big show, he says.

MYRON *(into phone)*. I don't care!

SALLY. Can't miss, he says. Twenty-one thousand, six hundred thirty-seven dollars …

MYRON *(into phone)*. Just find him!

SALLY. And forty-two cents.

MYRON. MA!

SALLY. I thought Dennam was out of town!

MYRON. He WAS out of town! He came back! It's like he picks up my scent!

SALLY. I didn't know you could smell mediocrity.

MYRON *(with a dismissive gesture, it saves time)*. Ehhh!

SALLY. Just like your father!

MYRON *(into phone)*. What? … Look, put Dennam on the phone! … Why? You wanna know why? All right. All right. I'll tell you why … Because I'm Myron Siegel, that's why! Whatyda say about that! … Hello?! … Hello?! *(Slams down receiver.)* Ehhh!

SALLY. How many times do I hafta tell ya, Myron, you don't have a name that keeps the conversation goin'.

(MYRON moves grumpily to the French doors. The main door flies open, and LITTLE WILLIE enters. He's a thug, but he is dressed a little too nattily. Not everything works sartorially. MYRON opens the French doors and looks outside.)

WILLIE. Boss, I got your message! Hi, Sally!

(SALLY just grunts and goes to the bar.)

MYRON. What took you so long?

WILLIE. The cabbie had the audacity to sneer at my tip. *(Shows brass knuckles, which he immediately pockets.)* I felt compelled to rebut.

SALLY. Rebut?

WILLIE. I learn a new word every day. That was Tuesday's. With a good vocabulary, I make the world a better place.

SALLY. You wanna make the world a better place?

WILLIE. I do.

SALLY. Get a new tailor.

MYRON *(looking down the street)*. Look at that! Lined up around the block at the Alhambra, empty sidewalk at the Regency.

WILLIE *(sees DAISY, likes what he sees)*. Hello, there.

DAISY *(likes what she sees)*. Hello, there.

WILLIE. They call me Little Willie.

DAISY *(still smiling)*. Why?

MYRON *(back into the room)*. Don't talk to him!

SALLY. Don't talk to him!

MYRON *(to WILLIE)*. Don't talk to her!

SALLY. Don't talk to her!

DAISY. Where's the privy, Uncle Myron?

MYRON. The what?

DAISY. Privy. We don't say bathroom in Buffalo.

WILLIE. That is very … genteel … of you.

DAISY *(beat)*. Well, my father is a Catholic.

SALLY *(points)*. That door, honey.

DAISY *(heads to door)*. Aw, this place is great! Ga-reat!!! *(Enters the bathroom and shuts the door.)*

MYRON *(to WILLIE)*. What do you hear about Carl Dennam? What's he up to makes everybody in town wanna see this show of his?

WILLIE. Nobody knows! That's the thing! It's the element of the … unknownness of the enterprise makes us all, you know … fraught.

SALLY *(fraught)*. Fraught? What's fraught?

WILLIE. You know. Like you. All the time.

MYRON. It'll never stop! Ever since *Bovine Ballyhoo* of 1922. Remember, Ma? Remember what Dennam did then?

SALLY. Of course I remember! There's nothin' hard about my arteries!

WILLIE. *Bovine Ballyhoo*?

MYRON. I put together a spectacular revue featuring the greatest overweight tap dancers in the country. *(Wistfully.)* What a cast I put together! Total weight first day of rehearsal was 7,694 pounds. Dennam found out about the show, set up a free buffet in an empty storefront across the street from the theatre the morning of opening night. Had a color poster of a big knockwurst in the window. Not one of my tappers walked past that knockwurst on the way to work without stopping in. That night, third chorus of "Alabany Bound," all my guys hit the down left platform at once, the platform collapses, they all end up in the pit. Nate Birnbaum, five eight, 325, went right through the kettle drum and tore his trapezius.

WILLIE. His what?

MYRON. It's a very important muscle. I don't wanna talk about it.

(WILLIE makes a note.)

MYRON *(cont'd)*. Next day, the buffet's gone, Dennam's gone, *Bovine Ballyhoo* is closed, I'm broke and 20 of the most graceful tappin' fat guys ever assembled are out of work. Same thing with *The Big Soak* of '26.

WILLIE. *The Big Soak*?

SALLY. A water ballet.

MYRON. Classiest thing you ever seen in a theatre. Fifty beautyful girls in bathing suits, Irving Berlin tunes, three swimming pools, diving boards … *(Gestures wistfully, remembering the girls.)* … bouncy diving boards … orchestra pit filled to the brim with water … *(Moved.)* … musicians in little boats. I'm weeping just thinking of it.

SALLY. There was a lot of weeping, trust me.

MYRON. Week before we open, Dennam books the theatre next door to *The Big Soak* for a new play—a sequel to *Ben-Hur*.

WILLIE. A sequel to *Ben-Hur*?

SALLY. *Ben-Him*.

MYRON. We didn't stand a chance.

WILLIE. Boy oh boy …

SALLY. *Coo Coo Ca Choo*!

MYRON. No. I can't talk about *Coo Coo Ca Choo*.

WILLIE. Come on, boss.

MYRON. No.

SALLY. Tell 'im.

MYRON. No!

SALLY. Tell 'im.

MYRON. No!!

SALLY. Tell 'im.

MYRON. Homing pigeons! I found a guy had homing pigeons would fly anyplace and back, on a cue from a bassoon! It was colossal! My writer wrote a story about this accused murderer whose pigeons fly away at intermission, and come back at the climax with a note from the governor in the lead pigeon's beak just in time to save this guy from the electric chair!

WILLIE. What happened?

SALLY. Opening night Dennam steals the bassoon.

MYRON. We tried everything. Oboe. Trombone. French horn. Nothing.

SALLY. Lousy birds stayed offstage. Wouldn't work without the bassoon.

MYRON. Goddamn union pigeons!

SALLY. Myron! Relax! You'll live longer!

MYRON. What, that's supposed to be a good thing?

WILLIE. But why? Why does Dennam do this to you?

MYRON. Aw, he's just jealous! His old man was the same way! His old man was a producer just like my old man! And every time Pop came close to bringing a hit show to Broadway, Dennam's old man shot him down by producing something bigger himself at the same time! He lived to step all over my old man! Just like Dennam Jr. lives to step all over me!

WILLIE. Boss … I am … empathetic.

MYRON *(beat)*. Don't tell me your troubles! *(Grabs a newspaper.)* What about this dame, this Ann Farrow?

SALLY. Who?

MYRON. Says right here … *(Reads.)* "The only tidbit of information Dennam would reveal to scribes is that this new show features the New York stage debut of a smashing new actress, Ann Farrow."

WILLIE. Oh, yeah! There's been a modicum of discussion.

MYRON. So? What's the word on the street about her?

WILLIE. The little I could get was Dennam dragged her out of a roomin' house and took her off with him on a voyage.

MYRON. Voyage? What kind of voyage?

WILLIE. You know … *(With great meaning.)* A voyage! I understand it involves a boat. They get back, boom, she's the toast of Broadway.

MYRON. Just for gettin' on a boat with Dennam?

SALLY. She must have really known how to shiver his timbers.

MYRON. Shut up, Ma!

WILLIE. Boss, I never seen you this upset before.

MYRON. It was never 1933 before! I was never up to my ass in debt before! I never had a show that was guaranteed to keep me out of the poorhouse before! *Foxy Felicia*! What a story! What a score! And more dames than … than … sticks that you … shake! Now it's all going in the hopper!

SALLY. Along with my twenty-one thous …

MYRON. Shut up, Ma!

WILLIE. Aw, come on, boss! It's only one little show.

MYRON. One little show? Willie, let me ask you this. If you went to the box office today, as I did, and asked about the advance on tonight's opening, as I did, and learned, as I did, that because of Dennam's surprise show opening directly across the street from *Foxy Felicia*, because of that show, over 70 percent of our audience canceled, and proceeded across that street to purchase tickets for Dennam's opening, if you found all that out today, as I did, what would you do?

SALLY. I'd shit my pants.

MYRON. As I did!

DAISY *(has re-entered. Goes to her suitcase)*. Whoa! Shit! There's somethin' you don't hear in Buffalo!

MYRON *(to the heavens)*. Why me?

DAISY. Shit! That is so great! *(To SALLY as she lifts her suitcase.)* Where's my room, Grandma?

SALLY. I told you … I ain't your Grandma!

DAISY. You ain't?

SALLY. Not in Manhattan, I ain't!

WILLIE. I think Sally means that, uh, in the present circumstance, she wishes to keep her relationship with you … clandestine.

DAISY. Clandestine?

WILLIE. Furtive. Impenetrable. Like that.

DAISY *(to SALLY)*. You want me to be … impenetrable?

MYRON *(hasn't really been listening, but is now)*. Yes! At least till you get back to Buffalo!

SALLY. I may be your mother's mother, but I'm nobody's grandma! Call me Sally.

DAISY. Sally! That is great!

SALLY *(points)*. Take that room. There's a nice view of the Automat.

DAISY. Hot dog! *(Goes to the bedroom door and stops.)* Oh! Uncle Myron, I have a letter in my suitcase Ma wanted me to give you. *(Gets an envelope from her bag.)*

MYRON. Later, kid. I got a lot on my mind. *(Plops on the sofa and holds his head.)*

DAISY. Oh. OK. I'll just leave it here on the fruit. *(She tucks it into a fruit bowl, steps quietly over to MYRON then blasts in his ear.)* ARE YOU THINKIN' ABOUT SHOW BUSINESS?

MYRON *(startled then relaxes)*. Yeah. Show business.

DAISY. HOT DOG! *(She enters her bedroom and slams the door closed.)*

WILLIE. Hey, boss, who's the little cutie?

MYRON. My sister's kid. Daisy. She wants to be an actress. I'm supposed to set her straight and send her back home. My luck, she decides to land here today!

WILLIE. She's somewhat enchantin'.

MYRON. You keep away from her!

SALLY. Yeah! Hands off!

MYRON. She ain't been … indoctrinated!

WILLIE. Oh. *(Beat.)* I don't think I even have to look that up.

MYRON. Stay away!

SALLY. Have you told your loving wife about her yet?

MYRON. No. She don't even know I have a niece. But she'll be fine. Bertrille is very family oriented.

SALLY *(nudges WILLIE)*. Yeah. Like the Borgias.

MYRON. Shut up, Ma. Willie … think! We gotta do something about Dennam!

WILLIE. But, boss, you got a big musical show with dames and legs and scenery and … dames! Dennam probably just has another one of his home movies about animals.

MYRON. If you'd read a paper, you'd know that whatever Dennam's got, it ain't no home movie! *(Back to newspaper.)* Look … "DENNAM'S STUNNING SURPRISE." Listen to this … *(Reads.)* "Carl Dennam has a secret, and he's not telling. The famed nature picture maker has kept a tight lid on his new production at the Alhambra, but says that the audience will see something spectacular, something mind-boggling. Dennam says the show will be the biggest hit in Broadway history!"

WILLIE. But, boss, how did this happen? I thought the Gershwin show was goin' into the Alhambra.

MYRON. Dennam wanted it, Dennam got it.

WILLIE. Over Gershwin?

SALLY *(to MYRON)*. Tell 'im.

MYRON. Ma …

SALLY. Tell 'im. *(Nothing from MYRON.)* All right, I'll tell 'im. *(To WILLIE.)* Dennam owns the Alhambra.

WILLIE. You're kiddin'! I didn't know he had that kinda dough.

SALLY. He inherited the theatre from his father.

MYRON. Ma …

SALLY. Who won it in a poker game …

MYRON. MA …

SALLY *(indicates MYRON)*. From HIS father!

MYRON. MA!

SALLY. The late Arnold R. Siegel, producer!

MYRON. Dennam's out to get me again! All he has to do is fart out a cockatoo and a mongoose, and they line up for 20 blocks! I've been avoiding Higginbottom all day. As soon as he finds out about this, he'll pull all his money out of the show! I know it! *(To WILLIE.)* Look, Willie, I want you to get over to the Alhambra and find out anything you can about that show! I just gotta stop Dennam before he destroys me!

WILLIE *(shows brass knuckles)*. Boss, I will do my utmost. *(Starts for the door.)*

SALLY. And keep that hardware in your pants!

WILLIE *(stops at the door)*. Straight lines. Everywhere I go, nothin' but straight lines.

(As WILLIE reaches the door, it opens, and BERTRILLE SIEGEL enters. She is a bit younger than MYRON and very beautiful.)

WILLIE *(cont'd)*. Hi, Mrs. S. You're looking exquisite, as per usual.

BERTRILLE *(not terribly enthused)*. Willie …

WILLIE. If you'll allow me to beg your pardon, I will … exeunt.

BERTRILLE. What?

WILLIE. Learned that one last week. It's from Shakespeare. *(Reacts to what he perceives is ignorance.)* He's a writer! *(Shaking his head, he leaves, closing the door behind him.)*

BERTRILLE *(moves to embrace MYRON in a shallow greeting)*. Myron, darling! Are you all right, sweetheart?

MYRON. I have no reason to live.

BERTRILLE *(there is no listening involved)*. Uh huh. Do you have any idea what Dennam is up to?

SALLY. I'll tell you what I'm up to—twenty-one thousand …

(MYRON looks at her.)

SALLY *(cont'd)*. Yeah, I know. Shut up, Ma.

MYRON. Where you been?

BERTRILLE *(posing)*. I've been at the salon at Hattie Carnegie preparing myself to be put on display at your opening.

MYRON. Well, you wasted your time and my money.

BERTRILLE. Oh, Myron, don't be silly.

MYRON. Silly! Ha! If I can't figure somethin' out in the next two hours, I'll have to cancel the opening!

BERTRILLE. Really?

MYRON. Really.

BERTRILLE. Hmm.

MYRON. Hmm? Whatyda mean hmm?

(The telephone rings, and MYRON answers it.)

MYRON *(cont'd)*. Siegel! … What? … Where? … Now? … All right, stall him a coupla minutes … What? … I don't know, tell him he makes the best yo-yos in the civilized world. He loves talkin' about his yo-yos. Just stall him! All right! *(Hangs up the phone. Angrily.)* Higginbottom!

SALLY. Do you think he knows?

MYRON. Of course he knows! He's an idiot, but he knows!

SALLY. Well, he can't pull out now, can he?

MYRON. He can't pull out what he's spent, but he sure as hell can pull out what's left! So both of you be nice to him!

(SALLY and BERTRILLE react with a vocal "Eww!")

BERTRILLE. I can't be nice to him. That … wig disgusts me.

MYRON. Don't mention the wig! He thinks nobody knows!

BERTRILLE. He thinks nobody knows?

SALLY. It looks like one of your pigeons.

MYRON. Ma …

SALLY. Sitting on the toilet.

MYRON. Ma …

SALLY. A constipated pigeon.

MYRON. Ma!

(Long beat, SALLY and MYRON lock stares. She takes a sip from her drink. Then she speaks, because she can't resist.)

SALLY. Sitting on the toilet.

MYRON. MA!

SALLY *(rises)*. I'll be in my bedroom.

MYRON *(races to stop her)*. No! You stay! You, he likes!

SALLY. Which explains my exeunt.

MYRON *(pulls her back towards the chair)*. He likes you. It's good for me that he likes you. You know how I know he likes you?

SALLY. Let me guess. The drooling?

MYRON. Because he told me he likes you! And the drooling.

SALLY *(indicates BERTRILLE)*. Let Eleanora Duse entertain him. She's lookin' for work since you didn't give her the lead in *Felicia*.

BERTRILLE *(hurt)*. I would have been magnificent!

MYRON. You're too pretty.

BERTRILLE. What does that mean?

SALLY. It means you're too old.

BERTRILLE. At least when I'm onstage I keep my clothes on.

SALLY. As opposed to the casting sessions …

BERTRILLE. Well, I never …

SALLY. That's not what I heard.

MYRON. Ma!

(BERTRILLE huffs off to her bedroom, slamming the door behind her.)

SALLY. Why you stay with her, I'll never know.

MYRON. She loves me.

SALLY. Prove it.

MYRON. She married me!

SALLY. She thought she was marrying a wallet!

MYRON. Baloney.

SALLY. She's a talking tumor.

MYRON. Knock it off …

SALLY. She spends every nickel you make. She steams open all your mail before you read it.

MYRON. You're dreamin' …

SALLY. She flirts with anything with facial hair …

MYRON. Please …

SALLY. Except my sister Rose …

MYRON. Ma! Concentrate! Please! Make Higginbottom happy!

SALLY. What kind of a name is that, anyway? Sig Higginbottom.

MYRON. He had a Hungarian mother and a Limey father. Strange bedfellows.

SALLY. Yeah, well my bed ain't strange enough for that fella.

MYRON. I'm tellin' ya, Ma … play ball … or come a week from Tuesday … *(Ominously.)* I'm sendin' ya back!

SALLY *(beat)*. You wouldn't dare!

MYRON. Try me!

SALLY. Myron …

MYRON. Be nice to him or you're goin' back to strippin'!

SALLY. I can't strip anymore! Look at me!

MYRON *(beat)*. OK, maybe not in New York! But Jersey!

SALLY. Damn it, Myron!

MYRON. If Higginbottom pulls the plug, we're busted. Twenty-one thousand, six hundred thirty-seven dollars …

SALLY. *(beat)*. You owe me, sonny boy.

MYRON. And forty-two cents.

SALLY. You owe me big time! *(Heads to a chair.)* I told your father. I told him it was your sister Louise who should have been the producer.

MYRON. Louise hated show business.

SALLY. So what? At least she had a brain.

MYRON. I got a brain!

SALLY. Hers is in her head! *(Sits.)*

(DAISY comes out of the bedroom, wearing a robe with her hair up. She heads for the bathroom. The doorbell rings.)

DAISY. Wow! That ain't a bedroom, it's a small country! *(She opens the bathroom door, steps in and out again.)* And we are talkin' TUB!

(DAISY enters the bathroom and slams the door. MYRON goes to the main door and opens it. There stands SIG HIGGINBOTTOM. He is in his 60s, has a middle European

accent, but there are traces of Dad in his vocabulary. He is dressed for the opening. He also sports the worst toupee in captivity.)

HIGGINBOTTOM. I szay … I hef a bone to pick vid you.

MYRON. Sig, come in!

HIGGINBOTTOM. Vee are schnookered! I'm chust comink from da box office, and …

MYRON *(to SALLY)*. Look! Mr. Higginbottom!

HIGGINBOTTOM *(turns around)*. Vhere?

MYRON *(turns him back)*. No! There! My mother!

HIGGINBOTTOM. Oh, Zally! You look luffly tonight! How are you?

SALLY. Happy as a pigeon!

HIGGINBOTTOM. Dat's nice.

SALLY *(under her breath)*. Sitting on a toilet.

MYRON *(stifled)*. Ma!

HIGGINBOTTOM. Excuse me?

MYRON. Nothing! Nothing, Sig. Well! Nice talking with you! Thanks for dropping by! *(Leads him to the door.)* I'll see you over at the theatre …

HIGGINBOTTOM *(accommodating)*. Yes! Yes, tank you … No! *(Walks back into the room.)* No … vee hef a sticky vicket … Da box office is, how you say … *(Makes raspberry noise.)* Kaput! Da mongoose man. Dere all going to see dat show. You knew dis?

SALLY. He knew dat.

MYRON. Ma! *(To HIGGINBOTTOM.)* Yeah, Sig, I'm workin' on that now.

HIGGINBOTTOM. How are you vorking on dat? Dere already gone … *(Raspberry again.)* cross da street. Nobody coming to my *Felicia.* Everybody going to da mongoose!

MYRON. I'm tellin' ya, Sig, I've already swung into action.

HIGGINBOTTOM. You've svung?

MYRON. Yep.

HIGGINBOTTOM. How hef you svung?

MYRON. The wheels are turning!

HIGGINBOTTOM. Are you svinging or vheeling?

MYRON. I'm swingin', I'm wheelin'! By midnight tonight I'll have this completely under control.

HIGGINBOTTOM. Vell, dat would be a good ting because by midnight tonight, if she's not under control, me and my checkbook vill be … *(One more raspberry.)* on da first boat back to Budapest!

MYRON *(leads him to the door)*. Trust me, Sig. Hey! Why don't you and Sally grab a little supper while I figure this thing out?

HIGGINBOTTOM *(enthused)*. Zupper vid Zally?

SALLY. Oh, Jesus …

HIGGINBOTTOM. Zay!

SALLY. Uh … I think … I have … to … go to the privy and … powder … my entire body. *(Heads off.)*

MYRON *(stops her)*. Come on, Ma! Mix a little food in with that bourbon!

HIGGINBOTTOM. Zally … I vould be honored.

SALLY. Well, I'm not sure, I …

MYRON *(aside, to SALLY, acting it out)*. Boomp-boomp-pa-boomp-boomp-pa …

SALLY. Fine. *(Grabs her coat. Aside to MYRON.)* You owe me …

HIGGINBOTTOM. I vill tell you all about my yo-yos.

SALLY *(aside, to MYRON)*. Big time.

MYRON *(aside)*. Put it on my tab, Ma. *(To HIGGENBOTTOM.)* So, Sig. Are we Jake?

HIGGINBOTTOM *(to MYRON)*. No! I am Zig. You are Zeigel! And by midnight tonight, Zeigel gets it svung! Or else … *(One raspberry for the road.)* Bops your uncle!

MYRON. Don't you worry about a thing. Hey, you kids have a swell time! And, hey! *(To SALLY.)* After dinner, why don't you accompany Sig to *Foxy Felicia*!

HIGGINBOTTOM *(delighted)*. Oh, ho!

SALLY *(aside, to MYRON)*. I will kill you.

MYRON. Great! I'll see you after the show! *(Starts off.)* I need to talk to Bertrille … *(Exits to their bedroom.)*

SALLY *(to HIGGINBOTTOM)*. Look, give me 15 minutes, will ya, Sig? I gotta … *(Sweeps three bottles off the bar.)* prepare myself for the occasion. *(Heads to her bedroom.)*

HIGGINBOTTOM. Yah! Yah, of course. I'll be back in 15 minutes! *(At the door.)* What rapture! What choy! Zupper vid Zally! *(He is gone.)*

SALLY *(at her bedroom door, with disgust)*. I'm gonna be zick. *(She goes into her bedroom and closes the door.)*

MYRON *(enters from the bedroom with BERTRILLE)*. All right, look … Ma's gone out to dinner with Sig … I'm going down to the barber shop in the lobby. If anybody knows what Dennam is up to, it's Dooley. *(Going to the door.)* If Little Willie calls, write down everything he tells you.

BERTRILLE. Oh, Myron, you're getting all excited over nothing. *(Goes to the mirror and adjusts her hair and make-up.)*

MYRON *(builds dramatically)*. I don't think so. I think this is it. I think this is my Big Life Moment. Pop said to me once … "Nothin' comes easy. Success is somethin' you gotta earn. And you gotta be ready when your Big Life Moment comes." Well, Pop never got a break. Never got his Big Life Moment. But I'm gettin' mine. This is it. It's me against Dennam. Dennam's takin' nothin' else from me! Nothin'! I gotta beat him. I just gotta. For Pop!

BERTRILLE *(turns away from mirror)*. Hmm? Did you say something, darling?

MYRON *(heads to the door)*. Never mind.

BERTRILLE *(runs to the door, meets him)*. Be careful, my love! I worry about you so, so much!

(They kiss. MYRON heads for the door. BERTRILLE waits a beat after he closes the door, then she races to the phone and slaps the bar for the hotel operator. Her sweetness disappears.)

BERTRILLE *(cont'd)*. Give me backstage at the Alhambra Theater … No, I don't know the number. Don't people like you look up numbers? … Then look it up! *(Paces a moment.)* Yes? … Thank you … I'd like to speak to Mr. Dennam … Don't tell me he's indisposed! *(Whispers loudly.)* You tell him "Tushie" wants him, and she wants him right now! You heard me. Tushie.

(The main door opens. MYRON re-enters. BERTRILLE is taken aback. She hides the receiver behind her back. MYRON goes to the desk, rummages in the drawers and finds what he's looking for.)

MYRON *(heads back to the door)*. Need some show tickets. To pass around at Dooley's. Get some fannies in the seats. *(Stops.)* What's the matter?

BERTRILLE. Nothing.

MYRON. There's a … thing in the room. A nervous … thing.

BERTRILLE. I'm nervous about you, sweetheart. You know that.

MYRON. That's it? The nervous is just the usual me makin' you nervous nervous?

BERTRILLE. Yes. Go.

MYRON. Christ, I hope Dooley knows what Dennam is up to.

(MYRON leaves. BERTRILLE hears a voice through the phone.)

BERTRILLE *(into the phone).* Dennam? … Ha! … I knew "Tushie" would get your attention! … I haven't heard from you in a month and I want to know what the hell you're doing over there … What? It's all part of what plan? … How is this new show of yours going to get me into *Foxy Felicia*? … What do you mean it's not really a show … If it's not really a show then why is everyone on Broadway going bananas? … What's so funny? Look, if you ever want to see me naked, you'll tell me everything and you'll tell me now! … *(Grabs the newspaper.)* What about you and this … Ann Farrow? … What? … Oh … Oh, really? And in all that time out on the ocean, you never sneaked into her cabin to swab her deck? … Well, you'd better swear or you'll never book passage on this dreamboat … What? … I told you, I am not leaving Myron until I'm absolutely certain you've taken over *Foxy Felicia*! … Well, this show of yours better do it! I want that part! And I will not play second fiddle to little Annie Farrow! … What? … No, I don't want to see your attraction … Oh, I'm sure your attraction is enormous … but Dennam, I don't care! Just get me what I want, and you'll get what you want …

(DAISY comes out of the bathroom, still in her bathrobe with her hair up, unseen by Bertrille, who gets syrupy.)

BERTRILLE *(cont'd).* Well, of course your little Tushie woves you! You know that Denny Wenny! … Yes … I'll see you tonight … when it's all over! … Bye-bye, Denny Wenny … Tushie says bye-bye … bye-bye now … bye-bye … bye-bye … *(Hangs up.)*

DAISY. Hi!

BERTRILLE *(turns and sees DAISY)*. JESUS! *(Composes herself.)* Mary and Joseph!

DAISY. Whew. I almost never get all three!

BERTRILLE. How long have you been standing there?

DAISY. Just this second.

BERTRILLE. Who are you?

DAISY. Daisy! I'm from Buffalo!

BERTRILLE. What … are you doing here?

DAISY. Uncle Myron told me I could come here anytime I want.

BERTRILLE. Uncle … Myron?

DAISY. Yeah.

BERTRILLE. He knows you're here?

DAISY. Yeah. He picked me up at the bus station. He's just the sweetest guy in the whole world and he's gonna help me get into show business!

BERTRILLE. Oh, he is, is he?

DAISY. Yep. And I told him that if he helped me get into show business, I'd do anything he wanted me to do!

BERTRILLE. I bet you did.

DAISY. Is Uncle Myron helping you get into show business too, Tushie? You look like the type.

BERTRILLE. Oh, no … no … listen …

DAISY *(goes to the fruit basket, leaves a towel on the table)*. Oops. Uncle Myron still hasn't read Ma's letter. *(Takes it.)*

BERTRILLE. Ma?

DAISY. My mother. His sister.

BERTRILLE. Myron has a sister?

DAISY. Yeah. That's how he got to be my uncle. Oh, well. He'll get to it. He's a busy man in show business. *(Puts the letter back on the fruit.)*

BERTRILLE. So, then, you really are …

DAISY. Hey, you know, Tushie … I'd love to chat. But I'm still kinda wet. Do you mind?

BERTRILLE. Not at all.

DAISY *(as she heads to her room)*. Tushie! What a great name! *(Stops, looks back.)* And you know … it FITS! *(Enters her room and slams the door.)*

(BERTRILLE zips to the fruit, takes the letter, discovers that it is not sealed, opens it and reads.

Almost instantly, she realizes that the letter is VERY IM-PORTANT. Her eyes bug out, and her jaw drops. She finishes reading in astonishment.

DAISY's door opens. She's coming back for her towel. BERTRILLE stuffs the letter back into the envelope and tries to conceal it, but DAISY steps into the room and sees the envelope.)

DAISY *(cont'd, pleasantly)*. Whoa! Tushie! Bit of a Nosy Nellie, there, aren't ya! *(Grabs the envelope.)* Back in Buffalo, we call these kinda things "occasions of sin!" I'll just remove the temptation, there, Tush!

(DAISY keeps the letter, goes happily back into the bedroom and slams the door shut. BERTRILLE, very frustrated, goes briskly to her bedroom and slams that door shut.

As her door slams shut, the main door opens, and MYRON comes in again. He goes directly to the phone, lifts the receiver and taps the bar.)

MYRON *(into the phone)*. Yes, this is Mr. Siegel in room 621. Why is the barber shop closed? … What? … Since when does Dooley work for Dennam? … What leading man? … Well, give me a name? … Hello? … Damn! *(He slams the receiver against the table with each "damn.")* Damn, damn, damn, damn, damn! *(He hangs up.)*

(BERTRILLE enters from her bedroom with a feather boa wrap for her shoulders.)

BERTRILLE *(taken aback)*. Myron! I thought you were going to the barber shop!

MYRON. Dooley closed early.

(SALLY emerges from the bedroom with three empty bottles.)

MYRON. I thought you were out with Sig!

SALLY *(going to the bar)*. I got nine minutes. I'm savoring each one. *(Dumps bottles in waste basket.)*

MYRON. Get this! Dooley. The barber. He's workin' for Dennam! Dennam hired Dooley to do a trim job on his star! *(Indicates BERTRILLE's wrap.)* Where you goin' with the feathers?

BERTRILLE *(whips off the boa)*. I was going to the drug store, but I changed my mind. What star?

MYRON. The leading man! Whoever the hell he is. Nobody knows! It's this big secret!

SALLY. Well, why don't you just go over there and find out?

MYRON. I've been over there! Marquee's covered with this huge piece of canvas. Dennam's got two six hundred pound city cops at the stage door, keepin' people out. Cops the size of the Empire State Building.

(The door opens, and WILLIE bursts into the room. He wields a pistol and is towing a beautiful young blonde woman [ANN FARROW] with him. She is not pleased.)

WILLIE. Boss! You ain't gonna believe what I found out!

MYRON. Who's this?

WILLIE. In a minute. *(To ANN, using the gun.)* Sit.

ANN *(as she does, she whines)*. Ooh …

MYRON. What did you find out?

WILLIE *(pockets gun)*. It ain't a movie.

MYRON. What?

WILLIE. It ain't a movie. It's a monkey.

MYRON. A monkey!

SALLY. A monkey?

MYRON. Dennam's turned Broadway on its ear and all he's gonna give 'em is a monkey?

WILLIE. Boss, this ain't no regular monkey.

MYRON. What are you talkin' about?

WILLIE. Well, I turned on the charm with this dame who works in the box office.

MYRON *(points to ANN)*. Her?

WILLIE. No.

MYRON. So who's she?

WILLIE *(frenzied)*. In a minute! I'm talkin' about the monkey.

MYRON. What about the monkey?

WILLIE. Well, this dame heard one of the stagehands chattin' outside the little boys room and what she heard … whoo!

MYRON. Whoo? What whoo? Whoo what?

WILLIE. Well, first she heard 'em talkin' about Dennam shackin' up with some big actress unbeknownst to her husband.

MYRON *(to ANN)*. You?

ANN. Oh, I'm not that big.

MYRON *(to WILLIE)*. Who is she?

WILLIE. Not her. Somebody they call … Tushie.

MYRON. Tushie?

WILLIE. It's a nickname. Nobody knows who she really is.

BERTRILLE. My God.

MYRON *(to WILLIE)*. Tushie? *(To BERTRILLE.)* Your what?

BERTRILLE *(fast)*. Nothing.

WILLIE. So Dennam is shackin' up.

MYRON. OK, that's good. Anything I can get on Dennam that's bad is good.

WILLIE. But, boss, that's just the tip of the ice box …

MYRON. Oh, yeah, the monkey …

WILLIE. You gotta listen to me about this monkey!

MYRON. I'm listening! Tell me about the damn monkey!!!

WILLIE. I will! This dame heard one of the boys say "That's the biggest goddamn monkey I ever seen!"

MYRON *(after a beat)*. That's it? It's a big monkey? That's what she heard? Dennam's got a big monkey?

WILLIE. Boss, that ain't all …

MYRON. Then tell me all! Jesus!

WILLIE. Well, she heard one of 'em say … "I been in the trenches at the Marne, I stared in the face of von Kluck in Brussels, and I ran errands for Busby Berkeley, but nothin' I ever seen in my life is scarier than that big monkey."

MYRON. Scary?

WILLIE. Then she said these two guys beat it out the front door of the theatre. She asked them where they were goin' and one of 'em said, "the hell away from here."

MYRON. Because of a monkey? This whole mishegoss is over a monkey? What is so scary about a monkey?

ANN. It's a really big monkey.

MYRON. Who the hell are you?

WILLIE. Boss! Meet Ann Farrow!

MYRON *(rising)*. You're Ann Farrow?

ANN. Yes.

WILLIE. I see this tootsie walk out the stage door at the Alhambra. Her blondness and … pulchritude makes me think she's the dame from the voyage. I ask her name, she complies. I … *(Taps gun in his pocket.)* invite her here to see you.

ANN. If Mr. Dennam finds out about this …

(BERTRILLE scoots to her bedroom door.)

MYRON. Where you goin'?

BERTRILLE. Uh … I have to make a call.

MYRON. What's wrong with this phone?

BERTRILLE. It's private. I have to call Hattie Carnegie. My … new girdle is … encroaching.

(She enters the bedroom as MYRON looks to WILLIE for help.)

WILLIE. "To advance gradually in a way that causes damage!"

MYRON *(to ANN, with dispatch)*. You're in this show Dennam's opening tonight?

ANN. Well, in a way …

SALLY. What do you mean "in a way?"

MYRON. What's the show about?

ANN. Oh, I've been sworn to secrecy. We all have.

MYRON. "We all have?" Who's "we all?"

ANN. Oh … Jack, the Skipper, the crew, everybody. Mr. Dennam demanded we not talk to anybody about … the attraction.

MYRON. The attraction?

ANN *(catching herself)*. The show! The show!

(DAISY sticks her head out of her door. She no longer has a towel on her head, but she is still in a robe. She wields the envelope.)

DAISY. Oh! Uncle Myron! You're back! Don't forget Ma's letter!

SALLY *(annoyed, indicating ANN)*. Daisy! Come on! We got a thing goin' here!

MYRON *(exasperated)*. Not now, sweetie … just …

DAISY. I know! On the fruit! *(Puts it there, looks around.)* Looks like Nosy Nellie is gone, so it's safe! *(Indicates the envelope as she goes to her bedroom door.)* Keep an eye on that? Will ya? *(Beat, sweetly.)* Willie? Will ya, Willie?

(Giggling and snorting, DAISY goes back into the bedroom and shuts the door.)

WILLIE *(beat, then to all)*. Alliteration!

MYRON *(to ANN)*. What's the attraction!!!

WILLIE. It's a monkey. I'm tellin' ya.

MYRON. What's Dennam payin' you?

ANN. What? Oh, well, Mr. Dennam has bought me lots of lovely dresses and shoes and …

MYRON *(dismissing)*. Dresses and shoes! You hear that, Ma?

SALLY. Clothing, he gives her!

MYRON. Baby, how would you like a job in a real show?

ANN. You mean, as an actress?

MYRON. Yeah, that's what you are, isn't it? An actress?

ANN. I … suppose.

(BERTRILLE returns from her bedroom.)

MYRON. So, there you go. Starting first thing next week, I'll give you a featured part in *Foxy Felicia*! Hundred a week.

ANN. Dollars?

BERTRILLE. What featured part?!

MYRON. Yeah, and you don't have to shiver nobody's timbers to get it, either!

ANN. What?

BERTRILLE *(annoyed)*. What featured part!

MYRON *(to BERTRILLE)*. I'll get the writer to come up with something. Felicia's innocent little sister, something like that. *(To ANN.)* You can play a virgin, can't you?

ANN. Oh, it's a religious play?

MYRON *(lets that land)*. Whatdya say?

ANN. Well, it does sound interesting, but …

MYRON. Good! It's a deal! Now, all you gotta do is tell me what Dennam is up to over there.

ANN. Oh! I couldn't do that!

MYRON. Come on! I'm offering you cash on the barrel head, baby! Fort Knox lettuce! I'm gettin' a writer's gonna make you a virgin! You gotta give me something!

ANN. No. I couldn't do that to Mr. Dennam. You see … he needs me.

MYRON. What do you mean he needs you?

ANN. Just that. Without me, the show cannot go on.

MYRON. What!

(The doorbell rings.)

MYRON *(cont'd)*. Who could that be?

BERTRILLE *(quickly)*. I don't know!

MYRON. Willie! Take the voyager into the bedroom. Make sure she keeps her trap shut!

WILLIE *(as he grabs ANN and moves towards BERTRILLE's bedroom)*. Come on, honey, we'll discuss the vast wonder of the sea! In you go! *(Admires her rear and speaks to MYRON.)* Nice stern.

(They are gone. MYRON goes to the door and opens it. HIGGINBOTTOM is there.)

MYRON. Sig!

HIGGINBOTTOM. Vhere is Zally?

SALLY. Here I am, Siggy! *(Goes to him.)* Listen, I think we'd better skip zupper. Sonny boy's wheels are turning! You don't want to miss that, do you?

HIGGINBOTTOM. His vheels? Vhat is heppening?

SALLY. Somethin' new every minute!

(The doorbell rings again)

SALLY *(cont'd)*. Right on cue!

(SALLY drags HIGGINBOTTOM to the sofa. MYRON moves to the door and opens it. CARL DENNAM is there. He is about MYRON's age, brusque and succinct. He is, of course, dressed to a fare-thee-well. As each addresses the other by his last name, there is dripping contempt in their voices.)

DENNAM. Siegel!

MYRON. Dennam! What are you doing here?

DENNAM. I got a tip this is where I'd find Ann Farrow.

MYRON. Who tipped you?

DENNAM. None of your beeswax! *(Tears into the room, bounds around.)* Where is she? Is she here?

MYRON. Look, Dennam, I wanna know what you got goin' on over there at the Alhambra.

DENNAM. I bet you would.

SALLY. Who do you think you are?

DENNAM. I think I'm the fella who makes your life miserable. Whatdya think about that?

SALLY *(to MYRON)*. Well at least he knows who he is.

MYRON. You got no right to sweep into town with one of your barnyard gimmicks and use your press agents to suck the air out of every other show on the street!

HIGGINBOTTOM *(rises)*. No right!

(SALLY yanks him back to the sofa.)

DENNAM. It's a free country, last time I checked. *(To BER-TRILLE.)* Has Ann been here or not?

MYRON *(before BERTRILLE can speak)*. Maybe she been, maybe she ain't.

DENNAM. Say, what's the big idea?

MYRON. The big idea is I know where your girl is, and if you want that information you gotta reciprocate.

DENNAM. I need that girl, Siegel!

MYRON. Yeah? What for?

DENNAM. For my show.

MYRON. Use the understudy.

DENNAM. There is no understudy! Not for her!

MYRON. Why not?

DENNAM. My star won't perform without her.

MYRON. Why not?

DENNAM. He just won't, that's all! I gotta have that girl and nobody else. Now, you tell me where she is.

(WILLIE comes out of the bedroom.)

DENNAM *(cont'd)*. She in there? *(Heads to BERTRILLE's bedroom door.)*

MYRON *(stops him)*. Tell me about your monkey, Dennam.

DENNAM *(beat)*. How did you find out about my monkey?

MYRON. I got my ways.

DENNAM. The girl? Did she tell you?

MYRON. The girl kept her mouth shut.

DENNAM. Show me the girl!

MYRON. Show me the monkey!

(DENNAM whips out a pistol.)

HIGGINBOTTOM *(hides behind SALLY)*. Ooh! Iss a gun! Da mongoose man hass a gun!

DENNAM *(as WILLIE reaches for his gun)*. No you don't! Give it!

(DENNAM extends his hand for WILLIE's gun. WILLIE places it in DENNAM's hand. DENNAM looks back at everybody.)

DENNAM. You want a look at my monkey, you buy a ticket like everybody else!

MYRON *(moves towards DENNAM)*. Why, you …

DENNAM. Stay where you are!

(MYRON freezes.)

DENNAM *(cont'd)*. Nobody moves! Get me? Now, where's the girl!! Talk fast, Siegel, or I'll make a lead pin cushion outa ya!

SALLY *(chuckling)*. A lead pin cushion …

(DENNAM points his gun at her, and she changes tone.)

SALLY *(cont'd)*. Lead pin cushion!

MYRON. Ma!

WILLIE *(to whomever)*. It's a metaphor.

DENNAM. Where's the girl!

MYRON. I … uh … I let her go! Ten minutes before you got here! I sent her back to the Alhambra!

DENNAM. Yeah?

MYRON. Yeah!

DENNAM *(to BERTRILLE)*. Yeah?

BERTRILLE *(hedging but trapped)*. Yeah?

(DENNAM points his gun at SALLY and HIGGINBOTTOM.)

SALLY & HIGGINBOTTOM. YEAH!

(MYRON shares a moment of concealed triumph with SALLY, who doesn't quite get what he's so thrilled about. BERTRILLE is situated so that she sees the envelope back on the fruit. Her eyes bug open again. Cagily, as the scene progresses, she slips the envelope off the fruit and holds it. She slyly wends her way towards the main door.)

DENNAM. Now listen to me, all of you, and listen good! I'm going back to that theatre and Ann Farrow better be there, or it's curtains for the lot of ya!

SALLY *(giggling again)*. Curtains …

(DENNAM aims gun at her again, and she speaks in a different tone.)

SALLY *(cont'd)*. Curtains!

DENNAM. Curtains!

BERTRILLE. The lot?

DENNAM. The lot! This monkey is the biggest thing that's ever happened to me, biggest thing that's ever happened to this town! He's worth millions! Millions, I tell you! I'm gonna get him out in front of an audience tonight, and I'm not gonna let anybody stand in my way! *(Nods to BERTRILLE.)* You!

BERTRILLE. What!?

DENNAM. The door!

BERTRILLE *(looks at door; definitively)*. Yes!

DENNAM *(beat)*. Open it.

BERTRILLE. Oh. *(Goes to the door and opens it.)*

MYRON. Not this time, Dennam! You're not gettin' me this time!

DENNAM *(moves toward the door but stops)*. Ha! Give up, Siegel! You and your old lady! The biggest losers on Broadway! I've had your number since the day I was born!

(DENNAM tosses WILLIE's gun back to him then exits, slamming the door. BERTRILLE goes to the door and opens it.)

MYRON. Where you goin'?

BERTRILLE *(envelope in hand)*. Uh … I want to … give him a piece of my mind!

MYRON. He don't need your piece! I just gave him my piece!

(MYRON laughs joyfully and begins to do a little celebration jig as SALLY watches quizzically.)

WILLIE *(to BERTRILLE, politely)*. Excuse me, Mrs. S … *(Takes the envelope from her.)* This must have been … mistakenly appropriated.

(He puts it in his coat pocket and exits to ANN's room. Reluctantly, BERTRILLE closes the door.)

SALLY. What's with the joy jumpin'?

MYRON. I got him! Finally! I got Dennam where I want him!

SALLY. Sure, and as soon as he finds out where you got him, you and YOUR CLOSEST RELATIVES turn into lead pin cushions!

MYRON. Aw, he was bluffin'! I got his leading lady, AND I got that dirt on him and that Tushie dame! I got him!

BERTRILLE. Myron, you should let that girl go! This is … kidnapping! I'll get her … *(Starts to her room.)*

MYRON *(stops her)*. It's self-preservation! And while I'm preservin' myself, I'm preservin' you, think about that, why don't ya!

BERTRILLE. Myron, you are so … Oh! *(She huffs off to another room.)*

MYRON. Now all I gotta do is get that monkey! Millions, he said! Did you hear him? Millions! I just gotta get that monkey!

SALLY *(gets drink)*. Good luck.

HIGGINBOTTOM. Vass is diss vid da monkey?

MYRON. And I'll use that girl to get him!

HIGGINBOTTOM. Vhat girl?

MYRON *(points)*. The girl in that room.

HIGGINBOTTOM. Vhat room?

MYRON *(points again)*. That room! That girl gets me the monkey!!

HIGGINBOTTOM. Vhat monkey?

MYRON. The girl is the key!

HIGGINBOTTOM. Vhat key?

MYRON. The key to the monkey!

HIGGINBOTTOM. Vhat monkey?

MYRON. I don't know vhat monkey! His show is a monkey! A big monkey!

HIGGINBOTTOM. Is like a turkey?

MYRON. No is not like a turkey! Is a monkey! A real monkey!

HIGGINBOTTOM. How vill you get diss monkey?

MYRON. Easy. I got the girl. I'll put her in *Felicia*. Without the girl, Dennam closes his show, sells me his monkey, cheap!

HIGGINBOTTOM. And vhen you get diss monkey, vhat do you do?

MYRON. That's the beauty part, Sig! I put the monkey in *Felicia* too!

HIGGINBOTTOM. Da monkey in *Felicia*? Vhere?

MYRON. I don't know … uh … the New Year's Eve scene at the Copa! We put him in a tux, give him a funny hat and a stick, and he can lead the band! Perfect! Millions, he said! We beat Dennam and guarantee ourselves a smash hit! Two birds! One stone! Ain't that a great idea, Sig!

HIGGINBOTTOM. Let me tink about diss. *(No beat.)* No.

MYRON. No?

HIGGINBOTTOM. No. As ideas go, dere is brilliant, dere is zo-zo, and dere is … *(Raspberry.)* Your idea is … *(Raspberry.)* I am goink now. I hef had da monkey talk up the hoo hoo. I zay now vhat I said before. By midnight tonight, *Felicia* must be a hit! If not … *(MYRON, this time, makes the raspberry sound.)* You're learnink! *(To SALLY.)* Zally! Zupper and da zshow. Talley ho!

SALLY *(ushers HIGGINBOTTOM to door)*. OK, Sig. I'll just be a minute. Wait in the hall.

HIGGINBOTTOM. Da hall?

SALLY. Yeah. I'll meet you at da helevator. Go!

   (HIGGINBOTTOM goes.)

MYRON *(screams)*. I GOT HIM! I FINALLY GOT HIM! *(Gets himself a drink.)*

   (SALLY moves to the closet, gathers her coat and moves to main door.)

SALLY. OK, look … I'll get Higginbottom outta your hair for as long as I can but … Myron … listen to me …

MYRON. This is it, Ma. I'm tellin' ya … this is it. My Big Life Moment! I'm gettin' my chance and I'm takin' it! To the day he died, Pop always told me I had to be ready when my Big Life Moment came. And I am, Ma! I am ready!

SALLY. Myron, your father was a wonderful man but the Biggest Life Moment he ever came up with resulted in you. I'm not saying that's a bad thing, but it speaks to his essential ineffectiveness. Stop thinking about your father, Myron. Listen to your mother. In my life, I have told you to do many things. You've been a good boy. You've always done what Mama has told you to do. But now … now I must tell you to do something I never thought I'd tell you to do. Probably no mother in the history of motherhood has ever told her son to do the thing I am about to tell you to do.

MYRON. What's that, Ma?

SALLY. Myron?

MYRON. Ma?

SALLY *(beat)*. Get that fuckin' monkey.

(SALLY leaves. BERTRILLE comes out of her room. MY-RON rummages through the desk. The rest of this scene moves like gangbusters.)

BERTRILLE. Myron, how long do you intend to …

MYRON *(to BERTRILLE)*. Wait. *(Yells.)* WILLIE!!!

BERTRILLE. What are you looking for?

MYRON. My binoculars …

BERTRILLE. Why?

(WILLIE enters with ANN.)

WILLIE. Yeah, boss?

MYRON. I want you to take blondie here to the theatre!

(MYRON continues looking through the room, in coat pockets, anywhere the binoculars might be …)

WILLIE. What?!

MYRON. Not his theatre! My theatre! The Regency! Tell Max I want her locked in the prop room till I get there! I gotta see what Dennam's gonna do when he finds out she ain't comin' back! *(To WILLIE as he points to the bedroom.)* See if my binoculars are in there!

(WILLIE runs off.)

ANN. You can't do this to me!

MYRON. You just watch! *(Looking.)* They gotta be around here someplace!

ANN. I'm hungry!

MYRON *(losing patience)*. She's hungry! All right! At the theatre. In the ice box in the prop room! There are cupcakes we use in the Copa scene. *(Looking for the binoculars, to BERTRILLE.)* Where'd you put them!!!

BERTRILLE. Me?

WILLIE *(re-enters)*. Not in there.

ANN. Cupcakes?

MYRON *(to ANN)*. Yeah! *(To WILLIE.)* From the Copa scene!

WILLIE. Copa cupcakes?

MYRON. Yes! Eat them!

WILLIE. Isn't that what they call the dancing girls in the scene? The Copa Cupcakes?

MYRON *(still looking, he stops, losing it)*. There are the dancing Copa Cupcakes, and there are the cupcake Copa cupcakes. She eats the cupcake Copa cupcakes! Get her outta here!

WILLIE. OK, Boss!

MYRON. Hide her good! If Dennam finds her, we're all dead!

ANN. Ooh …

BERTRILLE. Wait!

MYRON. What?

BERTRILLE. Let me do it!

MYRON. What?

BERTRILLE. Let me take her to the Regency. Dennam's got a gun. When he finds out she's not at the Alhambra, he'll come after you with blood in his eyes. You'll need Willie for protection.

WILLIE *(shows gun)*. She may be right, boss.

MYRON. That's not a bad idea.

BERTRILLE *(gets her coat)*. It's a wonderful idea! *(Grabs ANN.)* Come on, honey …

(BERTRILLE drags ANN to the main door.)

MYRON *(intercepting her)*. I can trust you with this?

BERTRILLE. Myron, I'm your wife. I know what you want. As your wife, I will do what you want. It is what a good wife does.

MYRON *(sees something beneath the sofa)*. Aha! *(Finds the binoculars, to BERTRILLE.)* All right! You bring her! And stay with her till I get there! We'll find out what Dennam's gonna do without the girl, and we'll be at *Felicia* for the curtain.

BERTRILLE. Good. Good. *(To ANN.)* Let's go. *(Beat, she stops.)* Myron?

MYRON. Yeah?

BERTRILLE *(dramatically)*. Goodbye … Myron! *(She goes.)*

MYRON *(to WILLIE)*. She's always auditionin'.

(DAISY comes out of the bedroom, now dressed for the evening, Buffalo-style.)

DAISY. Hi, Uncle Myron!

(MYRON heads to the bedroom for a coat.)

DAISY *(cont'd, to WILLIE, sweetly)*. Hiya, Willie.

WILLIE *(gives the envelope to DAISY)*. Takin' good care of it, per your request!

DAISY. Oh! Thanks!

(MYRON returns from the bedroom.)

DAISY *(cont'd, to MYRON)*. You want this letter from Ma now, Uncle Myron?

MYRON *(totally preoccupied, checking the binoculars)*. Uh … uh … not now, not now. Just hold on to it.

(She starts to put it on the fruit again. WILLIE stops her.)

WILLIE. Uh … not the best idea. You should be more … *(Hides it inside a vase.)* … surreptitious.

DAISY *(touched)*. Gee … thanks …

WILLIE. Think nuttin' of it.

DAISY *(moony)*. I won't.

MYRON. Come on, Willie. We're gonna plant ourselves on the roof of the Regency and watch Dennam put the "closed" sign on the Alhambra!

DAISY. Can I come?

MYRON. Uh … no, Sweetie, Willie and I have to go out and … uh … destroy a show. You stay here and listen to the radio. *(Grabs WILLIE and heads to the door.)*

DAISY. All right. By the way, where's the lady?

(DAISY turns on the radio.)

MYRON. What lady?

DAISY. The lady you're helping to get into show business.

MYRON. I'm not helping anybody get into show business.

DAISY. Except me!

WILLIE. Boss, we goin' or not?

DAISY. This lady was on the phone here when I was coming out of the tub.

MYRON. Oh. That was no lady. That was your Aunt Bertrille. She … stepped out for a minute.

DAISY. Aunt Bertrille?

MYRON. Yeah.

DAISY. Oh, I don't think so.

MYRON. OK, Willie.

DAISY. This lady had another name.

MYRON *(indicates the binoculars)*. We can use these on the roof …

DAISY. And she was talkin' to somebody named … uh …

MYRON. Perfect view …

DAISY. Denny!

WILLIE. OK, boss!

DAISY. Denny Wenny!

MYRON. You got our protection?

WILLIE *(shows his gun)*. Armed and ready!

(They are about to reach the door when WILLIE stops.)

WILLIE *(cont'd)*. Denny Wenny?

DAISY. Now what was her name … ?

MYRON *(drags WILLIE towards the door)*. I GOT HIM! I FINALLY GOT HIM!

WILLIE. Boss …

DAISY. Tushie! That was her name! Tushie!

(MYRON and WILLIE stop cold at the door. They look at each other.)

MYRON & WILLIE. Tushie?

(Then they look back to DAISY. DAISY sits in front of the radio, turns it on and smiles.)

WILLIE. Boss … you think … .?

MYRON. WE GOTTA GET HER!

(They tear out the door, slamming it behind them.)

DAISY *(at the height of her enthusiasm)*. I LOVE THIS PLACE! *(She plops onto the sofa, gleefully.)*

(Blackout. Radio music up.)

SCENE 2

(It is about a half hour later. DAISY lounges on the sofa and is talking on the phone.)

DAISY. Oh, Ma, you wouldn't believe this place! This city is what Buffalo would be if you stuck Rochester inside it and added taxicabs and prostitutes! … Oh, come on, now, Ma, don't yell at me just 'cause I'm gettin' sophisticated … What? … No, I haven't met Aunt Bertrille yet, just some lady named Tushie who's havin' an affair with a guy named Denny Wenny … That is, I THINK it's an affair. For all I know, she's just another prostitute … Ma … Ma, you gotta stop cryin' …

(The doorbell rings.)

DAISY *(cont'd)*. Oops, there's the doorbell! I gotta go! … Ma, don't worry about me! … I'm not gonna be a prostitute. I'm gonna be an actress! Everybody around here says that's a whole step up from prostitute!

(The doorbell rings again.)

DAISY *(cont'd)*. Bye!

(She goes to the door and opens it. There stands JACK DRISKEL, about 30, sweetly handsome, terminally sincere and dressed for the evening.

The following conversation is between two people who hear words but don't contextualize well.)

DAISY *(cont'd)*. Hello.
JACK. Hello.
DAISY. Hello.
JACK. Where's Ann?
DAISY. Who's Ann?

JACK. My fiancée.

DAISY. Oh. Congratulations.

JACK. Why?

DAISY. You're gettin' married.

JACK. I know.

DAISY. To Ann.

JACK. I know.

DAISY. If you find her.

JACK. Is she here?

DAISY. I don't know. Is Uncle Myron helping her get into show business?

JACK. Who's Uncle Myron?

DAISY. My uncle.

JACK. She's already in show business.

DAISY. Who?

JACK. Ann.

DAISY. Oh. Did Uncle Myron help her?

JACK. Who's Uncle Myron?

DAISY. My uncle. *(Beat.)* You wanna start over?

(JACK has had enough and bustles into the room.)

JACK *(very perturbed)*. Oh, I don't know what's goin' on! I was backstage watchin' the crew tighten the leg brace on the attraction, and they were testin' the lights in the theatre and all the flashin' was makin' the attraction madder and madder. He started yankin' his chains and growlin' somethin' awful. So the Skipper told me to go find Ann 'cause she knows how to calm the attraction down …

DAISY. What's the attraction?

JACK. Kong.

DAISY. What's a kong?

JACK. I can't tell you.

DAISY. Why not?

JACK. I swore.

DAISY. Oh. And you got in trouble?

JACK. For what?

DAISY. For swearin'

JACK. Uh …

DAISY. You can say "shit" around here all you want.

JACK. Shit?

DAISY. See? Anyway … go back to your story.

JACK *(beat)*. So I been up and down the block for a half hour lookin', and when I get back to the theatre, one of the stage-hands told me Mr. Dennam got a call to come to this hotel room here, and I figured Ann would be with him. He's always draggin' Ann around and sendin' her little notes. *(Pointedly.)* I don't like it when Mr. Dennam sends Ann notes.

DAISY. Mash notes?

JACK. Naw. Mr. Dennam don't look at Ann that way. *(Sourly.)* Just the attraction looks at Ann that way. *(Shivers in disgust.)* Anyway, is she here or ain't she?

DAISY. I don't think so … *(Beat.)* Wait a minute!

JACK. What?

DAISY. Wait a minute!

JACK. What?

DAISY. Is she a real classy dame?

JACK. Yeah?

DAISY. Really really gorgeous?

JACK. Yeah!

DAISY. I mean so gorgeous if you're a guy and she walks in the room your legs kinda buckle and your pants get a little snug?

JACK. Well … I like her.

DAISY *(turns away, sharply)*. Tushie!

JACK. Bless you.

> *(The main door flings open. MYRON and WILLIE fly into the room.)*

WILLIE. She musta made it back to Dennam at the Alhambra.

MYRON *(heads to the phone)*. My own wife! Stabbin' me in the back!

JACK *(to DAISY)*. Who are they?

MYRON *(to JACK)*. Who are you? *(Taps a bar on the phone.)*

DAISY. That's my Uncle Myron and his henchman.

WILLIE. Henchman?

JACK. Henchman?

MYRON *(into phone)*. Get me the box office at the Regency Theatre!

DAISY *(to WILLIE)*. That's what you are, ain't you?

WILLIE. I'm your uncle's … uh … executive associate. I am at his beck and call at all hours of the day or night. If the boss want's somethin' attended to, it is my duty and obligation to take what needs to be attended to and … uh … attend to it.

DAISY *(beat)*. So you're his henchman.

WILLIE *(exasperatedly)*. Yesssss.

MYRON *(into phone)*. I wanna talk to Larry!

DAISY. You're kinda cute for a henchman.

WILLIE. You're kinda cute for a … Buffalonian.

JACK *(to DAISY)*. You're a Buffalonian?

WILLIE. Who are you?

JACK *(with a milking gesture)*. I always wondered … how do you milk one of them things?

WILLIE *(to DAISY)*. Who is he?

JACK. Never mind who I am. Where's Ann?

MYRON. Ann?

DAISY. Tushie!

JACK. Bless you.

MYRON *(into the phone)*. Larry! It's Siegel! Has my wife been over there? … *(Shakes head "no" to WILLIE.)* What?! *(Slams down the phone, to WILLIE.)* Forty more cancellations! *(To JACK.)* What do you know about Ann?

DAISY. Ann's his fiancée.

MYRON. Yeah?

JACK. Yeah!

DAISY. Yeah! And he found out she was here, so he come lookin' for her!

MYRON. Yeah?

JACK. Yeah!

DAISY. Yeah! This fella Dennam keeps givin' Ann notes, and he doesn't like that. Do ya?

JACK. I hate it!

DAISY. He HATES it! This Dennam treats Ann real bad!

MYRON. Yeah?

JACK. Yeah!

DAISY. Yeah! But Uncle Myron, I think Ann is …

MYRON. Wait! …

DAISY. Tushie.

JACK. Bless you.

MYRON *(to JACK)*. Listen, Jack, you mind if I ask you a question?

JACK. Go ahead.

MYRON. First of all, what's your name?

JACK. Jack.

MYRON. Jack? Your actual name is Jack?

JACK. Well, yeah. I thought you knew that.

MYRON. What made you think I knew that?

JACK. You just called me Jack.

MYRON. I call any fella I don't know Jack.

JACK. Oh. Well. Glad it worked out.

MYRON *(beat)*. Listen, Jack, where do you fit into this whole scheme?

JACK. Me? Oh. I'm the First Mate.

WILLIE. Oh the boat!

MYRON. The boat that made the voyage!

WILLIE. Where Dennam found the monkey!

JACK. You know about Kong?

MYRON. Who's Kong?

DAISY. Kong must be the monkey!

JACK. Kong is the monkey.

MYRON. What kinda monkey?

DAISY. He can't tell you.

MYRON *(to DAISY)*. Why?

DAISY. He got caught swearin'.

MYRON *(to JACK)*. Why?

JACK. I gave my word I wouldn't tell.

MYRON. To who? Dennam? You gonna keep your word to him after the way he's treated your girlfriend?

JACK. Girlfriend? Ha! We're getting married in the morning!

MYRON. All the more reason to stick it to Dennam! How dare he give her all those notes! You're her fiancée! You should be giving her notes, not him!

JACK. Well … yeah!

DAISY. Yeah!

MYRON. Yeah! Tell us what you know!

JACK. Who does he think he is!

MYRON. Come on, Jack! Spill it!

DAISY. Spill it, Jack!

MYRON. What's the big secret? What kinda monkey is Kong?

JACK. Why, I oughta …

WILLIE. Tell us, Jack!

MYRON. Yeah! Tell us, Jack! Tell us!

   (They all ad-lib coaxing JACK to spill it!)

JACK *(beat. Then he blurts)*. Kong is a gorilla!

DAISY. A gorilla?

JACK. Very big gorilla!

MYRON. How big?

JACK. Big as they come!

WILLIE. And how big would that be?

JACK. Thirty, 40 foot tall, at least.

   (Beat. MYRON, WILLIE and DAISY look straight ahead, slowly to the sky and collapse into the sofa.)

MYRON. Forty feet! Carl Dennam has put a 40-foot gorilla onstage at the Alhambra?

JACK. Mostly onstage. *(Illustrates.)* When he crouches, his rear end kinda sticks out on the loading dock.

   (The doorbell rings.)

MYRON. I'll get that! Look, Jack, I want you to wait in here … *(Leads him to the door of the den.)*

JACK. But what about Ann?

MYRON. I'll find Ann, and as soon as I do, I'll bring her to you.

JACK. You promise?

MYRON. I promise.

*(MYRON shoves JACK into the den and closes the door.
WILLIE and DAISY are getting comfy on the sofa.)*

MYRON *(cont'd)*. This guy can help us!

(The doorbell rings again.)

MYRON *(cont'd)*. Coming! *(Aside to WILLIE.)* Keep him
company, eh! *(Pulling WILLIE away from DAISY.)* While
I see who this is. Find out everything you can about the
voyage and the monkey.

WILLIE. Gotcha, boss! *(Goes into the den and slams the door.)*

DAISY *(as MYRON heads for the door, desperately sincere)*.
Uncle Myron!

MYRON. Yeah, sweetie?

DAISY. What the heck's goin' on?

MYRON. Did Jack tell you anything about the monkey?

DAISY. Not much. Just that it got real upset when they turned
the lights on and off in the theatre.

MYRON. Upset? Upset how? What did he do?

DAISY. I don't know. Whatever a gorilla does when he's
mad, I suppose. Maybe, you know, like …

*(DAISY provides him with a quick, looney, angry gorilla im-
itation. She ends up in a gorilla pose, standing on the sofa.)*

MYRON. Wait … Wait … that's it!

DAISY. It is?

MYRON. Well, it's part of it. You gave me an idea!

DAISY. So I helped?

MYRON. In a way, yeah.

DAISY. Hot dog! *(Plops onto the sofa.)*

*(The doorbell now rings and rings and rings. MYRON
rushes to the main door.)*

MYRON. I'm comin', damn it!

(MYRON opens the door. SALLY enters, breathless.)

SALLY. Myron! Myron! Big trouble!

MYRON. You don't know the half of it! Where's your room key?

SALLY. I think I drank it.

MYRON. Where's Sig?

SALLY. That's the big trouble. We went to the box office. With the cancellations, the advance for the opening is now 17. And that includes Sig's nine cousins from Romania who can't speak English. He blew his top! From the box office he called the boat. He booked passage at midnight for him and his checkbook. And maybe a couple of Romanians, I don't know. This is worse than when your father produced that all midget *Macbeth*.

MYRON. Ma …

SALLY. He got the actors for half price! Big deal!

MYRON. MA …

SALLY. You couldn't even see the witches over the pot!

MYRON. MA!

SALLY *(rants)*. Twenty-one thousand, six hundred …

MYRON. Where's Sig now?

SALLY. Picking up the boat ticket. He "vants to hef it in hiss hent!" I told him I'd meet him in the lobby at showtime. How's that girl?

MYRON. She got away.

SALLY *(not listening)*. Good. Well, at least with her we can … WHAT? How did she get away?

MYRON. Bertrille took her outta here! Bertrille betrayed me! With Dennam!

DAISY. Aunt Bertrille?

SALLY. I told you! I told you that bitch was gonna …

MYRON. Oh, Ma, don't start with the I told you now …

DAISY. I gotta meet that bitch!

SALLY. If we wanna get the monkey, we gotta get that girl back! Tell me you have a plan!

MYRON. I'm workin' on it!

DAISY *(to SALLY)*. Little Willie's grillin' the First Mate in the den!

SALLY. Good! What?

DAISY *(the only explanation she has)*. It's show business, Grandma!

(SALLY reacts.)

DAISY *(cont'd)*. Sally!

MYRON. Ma! I'm worried about that monkey!

SALLY. What are you worried about a little monkey for?

(WILLIE tears out of the den, heading for the bar. JACK also steps into the room but hangs by the door of the den, a little antsy. As this riff proceeds, WILLIE makes drinks for himself and JACK.)

WILLIE. How the hell did he get a 40-foot gorilla from that god forsaken island to 42nd Street?

JACK. Well, like I said, Kong has a thing for Ann.

SALLY. Wait a minute—the monkey's a 40-foot gorilla?

WILLIE. Boss, you gotta hear this guy's story!

MYRON. How could a monkey have a thing?

JACK. Oh, he has a thing, believe me. *(Beat. Everybody takes.)* For Ann. That's why we had to catch him.

SALLY. Who?

DAISY. Kong!

SALLY. Who's Kong?

DAISY. The gorilla!

SALLY. The 40-foot gorilla?!

WILLIE. How'd you do it?

JACK. Well … the natives kidnapped Ann and gave her to Kong as a sacrifice. I guess 'cause they were runnin' out of their own girls.

WILLIE. They kidnapped her!

JACK. Yep! *(To MYRON.)* Head?

MYRON *(beat)*. Pardon me?

JACK. Latrine.

DAISY *(whispers)*. Privy.

MYRON. Oh. *(Points.)* There.

JACK. Thanks. *(Goes to bathroom and closes the door.)*

SALLY. Who's Mr. Personality?

MYRON. The First Mate from Dennam's boat. I got Willie stallin' him. I figure I can use him to get Ann back here!

SALLY. Yeah? How?

MYRON. She's in love with this guy! All I gotta do is get him to bring her over here, I lock her in that room, Dennam loses his monkey and *Foxy Felicia*'s a hit!

DAISY *(desperately sincere)*. That might work!

SALLY. Are you in on this?

DAISY. I'm tryin'!

(The toilet flushes.)

JACK *(enters talking from bathroom)*. So everybody on the boat went to get Ann back. But by the time we got there, Kong had Ann in his paw and was walkin' back into the jungle. *(Heads into the den.)*

WILLIE. Holy Maroni!! … This big … ape … this gigantic … gorilla monkey thing … is walking into the jungle … with your fiancée … in his paw?

JACK. Well, he didn't know she was my fiancée at the time. If he had, I'd a been real mad.

(JACK takes a drink from WILLIE and goes back into the den. WILLIE follows, closing the door.)

SALLY. Look, Myron, even if you get that girl over here and lock her in, that still doesn't get you the monkey.

MYRON. If we only had Ann on our side. She could lure the monkey away from Dennam.

SALLY. What, he's a one-woman monkey? You can't get somebody else to lure him?

MYRON. He has the thing for Ann! Maybe he likes blondes, I don't know!

SALLY *(thinks, looks at DAISY)*. Myron?

MYRON. What?

(JACK enters from the den and goes to the bar to get ice or something for his drink. He just keeps talking. WILLIE hangs at the door of the den.)

JACK. Yeah! So we're walkin' and walkin', and we ain't findin' nothin', then, all of a sudden, Scabs falls into the big hole.

WILLIE. Scabs?

JACK. That ain't his real name. His real name is Bob. But we call him Scabs. Wanna know why?

EVERYBODY ELSE. NO!

JACK. Anyway, the big hole turns out to be a footprint!

DAISY. Kong's?

JACK. You get me now how big this fella is?

DAISY. Gotcha.

JACK *(heads back to den)*. Well, we fight our way through a big old lizard and a couple of dinosaurs, and …

SALLY. Hold the phone! Dinosaurs? You're crazy.

JACK. Ma'am, if you ain't walked in my shoes, don't try to lay claim to my socks. *(He enters the den.)*

WILLIE. This is spellbindin'! *(Follows JACK into the den.)*

SALLY *(again looking at DAISY)*. Myron!

MYRON. What?

SALLY. That wig your wife wore in *The Tasty Tart From Tucumcari* … where is it?

MYRON *(catching on)*. In her closet … I think.

SALLY *(stands DAISY up and examines her)*. Same height.

MYRON *(also examines DAISY)*. Same weight.

SALLY *(turns her around)*. Same stern.

MYRON. I'll look for the wig!

SALLY. I'll help!

> *(MYRON and SALLY rush off to his bedroom. DAISY is dazed. They slam the door shut as the den door opens. This time WILLIE heads for the bar for ice or something. JACK follows him, stands in the doorway and talks.)*

JACK. Finally, most everybody's dead from fightin' the over-size jungle creatures and terro-dactails and such, and it's just me alone, lookin' down on Kong's lair! And I hear Ann scream! *(He screams like ANN.)* Kong hears this scream too, and he runs like a madman towards this king-sized dinosaur.

WILLIE. Another dinosaur!

JACK *(getting progressively more animated)*. And this dino is creepin' up on Ann, but my trousers are caught up in some bramble and I can't do nothin'. So Kong grabs Ann away from the dino and sets her in the top of a tree. Kong takes a swing at the dino! Boom! Right in the kisser! Then the dino lifts up old Kong and slams him to the ground like a wrassler. Kong tries to get up but he falls backwards into

Ann's tree, shakin' her loose! Kong commences to boxin'
the dino, right, pow, left, pow, right, left, right, left! Then,
Kong takes the dino's head with his hands and holds him
by both jaws and yanks them apart. *(Demonstrates.)*

DAISY. Holy mother of God.

JACK. It weren't pretty. Then old Kong, once he knew he had
the dino's number, well, he upped and beat himself on the
chest. Like this. *(Demonstrates.)* Kong's kinda full of himself.

DAISY. What about your pants?

JACK *(beat)*. Ma'am?

DAISY. You were brambled.

JACK. Oh, yeah. Well, I unbramble my pants. I grab holda Ann,
and we take off like one of them fast-runnin' jungle cats!

DAISY. Cheetah?

JACK. No, ma'am, I grabbed her fair and square.

*(JACK heads into the den, and WILLIE follows. The bed-
room door opens then slams shut as MYRON and SALLY
rush out. MYRON is flailing a blonde wig.)*

MYRON. Got it!

SALLY. Try it on.

*(MYRON, juiced and not thinking, starts to put it on his
own head.)*

SALLY *(cont'd)*. Not on you! On her!

MYRON. Oh! Right!

*(MYRON and SALLY move to behind the sofa and cram the
blonde wig on top of DAISY's head. They rush around to the
front to survey their handiwork.)*

SALLY. Whatdya think? We fix up the wig, get her in a dress,
some flashy shoes, some jazzy make-up?

MYRON. If I was an ape, I'd go after her.

SALLY. Good! Now what?

MYRON. It's comin' to me … It's comin' to me … *(Moves to the den door.)*

SALLY. What? What's comin' to you?

MYRON *(yells into the den)*. Willie! Jack! Come here! *(To SALLY.)* I'll get a dress from Bertrille's closet …

(MYRON goes into their bedroom as JACK and WILLIE enter from the den, talking.)

JACK. So Dennam has us tossin' the bombs at Kong. Ka-boom! He's knocked out cold. Dennam says we're gonna build Kong a raft and bring him home as a side show, kind of. "He was king in his world," Dennam says, "but we're gonna teach him fear!"

WILLIE. What hubris!

(JACK shoots him a look. Beat.)

JACK *(moves to the bar)*. So we got Kong on the ship, stuffed him into steerage and brung him home.

WILLIE. Well, what happened when Kong woke up?

JACK. Dennam kept pumpin' him fulla some kind of medicine. Kong didn't wake up till this mornin'. Just after we put him in the chains on the stage.

MYRON *(enters and tosses a dress to SALLY)*. Here! Take her in your room and fix her up!

SALLY *(yanks DAISY toward her room)*. Come on, honey!

DAISY *(as she is whisked off)*. WAIT! *(Stops. To MYRON.)* Does this mean I'm in show business?

MYRON. Yes!

DAISY. Hot dog!

(DAISY and SALLY are gone.)

JACK. Now, I don't mean to be pushy or nothin', but I ain't seen hide nor hair of Ann yet.

MYRON. That's right, Jack. You haven't. And you know why you haven't seen Ann?

JACK *(beat)*. No.

MYRON. I'll give you a two-word answer, Jack. Carl Dennam.

JACK *(beat)*. What's the second word?

MYRON. Carl. Dennam. Jack.

JACK *(beat)*. OK, is that three words?

MYRON. CARL DENNAM!

JACK. WHAT ABOUT HIM?

MYRON. He's bad, Jack. Bad as they come. He finds these … these … innocent, unassuming, pure and virginal young women and … and … I can't bring myself to say it …

WILLIE. The boss is very sensitive.

JACK. What!? What does he do!?

MYRON. He … he manipulates them!

JACK. Yeah?

MYRON. Yeah!

JACK. He manipulates them?

MYRON. He manipulates them.

JACK. That ain't good.

MYRON. No, it ain't!

WILLIE. It's despicable!

JACK. I can't believe it!

WILLIE. Me neither.

JACK. He manipulates them! What's it mean?

MYRON. It means he takes these sweet, unexplored young things and hypnotizes them until they're … until they're rapt!

JACK. Wrapped?

MYRON. Yes! And then … then …

JACK *(growing angrier)*. He unwraps 'em?

MYRON. Yes! You must seek revenge!

JACK. Revenge?

MYRON. Of course! Dennam has taken the love of your life and set her up in a 32nd Street love nest with the biggest, hairiest John in the five boroughs! Just to make sure he becomes king of Broadway! Once he does, once the papers print the story, you'll get your fiancée back, that's for sure. But she'll be … damaged goods! Open your eyes, Jack! Ann is Kong's one night stand, and Dennam is Kong's pimp!

JACK. My God! What can we do?

MYRON. Help us, Jack! Help us bring Dennam to his knees!

JACK. But how!? How!?

MYRON. You gotta trust me!

WILLIE. Trust him, Jack!

MYRON. You gotta go over to the theatre and bring Ann back here!

JACK. Here?

MYRON. Where it's safe!

JACK. Where it's safe!

MYRON. Yes! *(Begins to nudge JACK to the door.)* And then … and then I have to get into the theatre myself.

JACK. Why?

MYRON. I'll explain later. Can you get me in?

JACK *(takes a couple of passes from his jacket pocket and hands them to MYRON)*. Well, I got a coupla extra passes …

MYRON. Great! So you do trust me?

JACK. No!

MYRON *(they have reached the door. Beat)*. Well … that'll come in time … Look, no matter what happens—don't tell Dennam about my plan. Got me?

JACK. Gotcha!

(MYRON shoves JACK out the main door. JACK re-opens the door.)

JACK *(cont'd)*. What plan?

MYRON. Exactly! Go! Rescue her, Jack! Rescue your damsel in distress!

(JACK looks at him quizzically.)

MYRON *(cont'd)*. Ann!

JACK. Oh. Right.

(MYRON shoves JACK out again and slams the door shut. Instantly, SALLY and DAISY enter from SALLY's bedroom. DAISY now looks very much like ANN.)

SALLY. Best I could do!

MYRON *(goes to the phone, taps for the operator and looks at DAISY)*. Gorgeous! Just … gorgeous!

WILLIE. I'll say!

(SALLY, the former stripper, illustrates to DAISY the fine art of female seduction.)

MYRON *(into the phone)*. Get me the Herald Tribune, please!

WILLIE. So what's the plan, boss?

MYRON. It came to me when Daisy mentioned the lights at the theatre.

DAISY. Hot dog!

MYRON. It's not gonna be easy. And you, young lady, are gonna have to be very, very brave!

DAISY. Hot dog! *(To SALLY.)* Is he talkin' to me?

MYRON *(into the phone)*. Get me Duffy in the news department. Yeah, the photographer. I'll wait. *(To DAISY.)* Jack said the lights flashing on and off, Kong had some difficulty, right?

DAISY. Right. Started yankin' his chains and growlin' somethin' awful.

MYRON *(into the phone)*. Yes! Is this Duffy? Duff … Myron Siegel! I've got a proposition, could be worth a few bucks to you … Can you meet me right away? … Good. At Lindy's. I'll be there in 15 minutes … Thanks, Duff! *(Hangs up.)*

SALLY. Myron! What's the scheme?

MYRON. I'll tell you at Lindy's. Daisy … you stay here and man the fort. *(Holds out his hand to WILLIE.)* Willie! Are you with me?

WILLIE *(beat. Puts his hand on top of MYRON's)*. Whatever it takes, boss!

MYRON. Ma?

SALLY. Twenty-one thousand, six hundred thirty-seven dollars … *(Puts her hand on.)* and forty-two cents.

MYRON. Daisy?

DAISY *(desperately enthusiastic)*. I have no idea what's going on!

MYRON. If you help me pull this off, it's your ticket to Broadway!

DAISY. Hot dog! *(Puts her hand on.)*

MYRON. Today, the monkey! Tomorrow …

DAISY. THE WORLD!

MYRON. What?

DAISY. Oh. Sorry. Thought that's where you were goin' with that.

MYRON *(breaks the handshake)*. C'mon!

(All except DAISY head for the door. MYRON stops and looks to the skies.)

MYRON *(cont'd)*. This is for you, Pop!

(SALLY and WILLIE exit.)

DAISY. Uncle Myron!

MYRON *(at door)*. What?

DAISY. Now what happens?

MYRON. Hey! You're in show business! I should think you'd know what happens now.

DAISY. Yeah? What?

MYRON. End of Act I! Blackout!

(He leaves, slamming the door behind him. DAISY quizzically faces front.

Blackout.

Note: if there is a curtain, MYRON says, "End of Act I! Curtain!")

END OF ACT I

ACT II

SCENE 1

(One hour later. DAISY paces anxiously around the room. She appears to be silently reciting something she's memorized. The radio is on. A commercial is being broadcast.)

COMMERCIAL ANNOUNCER. … So, remember, four out of 10 medical doctors recommend Shamrock Cigarettes for a smoother smoke. The kind of smoke that says "Top of the morning" to your lungs! So take a long drag to your health with Shamrock Cigarettes! Just look for the picture of St. Patrick lighting up on the label!

(As the broadcast continues, MYRON tears out of his bedroom, wielding a bracelet, heading for DAISY.)

DAISY. Uncle Myron, I'm memorizin' the big plan!
MYRON. Good!

(MYRON places the bracelet on DAISY's wrist and heads back to the bedroom, slamming the door. The radio continues playing as DAISY continues pacing and practicing.)

SHAMROCK SINGERS *(jingle, on radio)*. Shamrock, Shamrock, just take a puff.

Shamrock, Shamrock, can't puff enough.

Shamrock, Shamrock, give us a try …

It's worth the hack, so buy a pack.

You'll smoke us till the day you die!

(SALLY comes out of her room, hell-bent for the bar. She mixes herself a drink as the radio keeps playing, and DAISY keeps pacing.)

SALLY. You got the big plan?

DAISY. I'm just … full of it!

RADIO ANNOUNCER. And our final story this evening comes from the Great White Way where Carl Dennam, that Genius of the Jungle, opens his most spectacular show ever. Tell us about your show, Mr. Dennam!

(MYRON comes out of the bedroom and listens.)

DENNAM *(on radio)*. Oh, you'll have to see for yourself. All I'll say is that it'll be the greatest hit on Broadway, ever! And I'm not monkeyin' around! *(He laughs.)*

DAISY *(laughs)*. Ha! I get it!

(SALLY turns off the radio.)

MYRON. Is Willie back yet?

SALLY. No. Where is he?

MYRON. I sent him to find Jack.

SALLY. Do you think that Rhodes scholar was able to talk his fiancée into coming back here?

MYRON. We gotta hope. *(Points.)* My whole plan hinges on lockin' her in that room! *(To DAISY.)* Are you sure you understand everything, kid?

DAISY. You mean … *(Elaborately.)* The Big Plan! I sure do!

MYRON. OK! Repeat it to me! Exactly as I told it to you!

DAISY. Gotcha! *(Braces herself. Then, with increasing enthusiasm …)* Well … I'm … the fake Ann. *(She makes a "fake Ann" pose.)*

MYRON. Right!

DAISY. And you're hopin' Jack brings the real Ann back here so you can lock her in that room so she don't ball things up!

SALLY. Right!

DAISY *(to MYRON)*. And when the time comes for the real Ann to go onstage with the big monkey, I'm gonna go onstage with the big monkey instead because I'm … the fake Ann. *(The pose.)*

MYRON. Precisely!

DAISY. And then your friend Duffy is gonna have all his newspaper buddies flash all their cameras at the big monkey, and that'll make the monkey looney, and he'll yank off all his chains and bolts and make havoc in the theatre, and then I run out of the theatre yellin', "Here, Kong! Come and get it!" And because this monkey's a monkey he thinks I'm the real Ann even though I'm the fake Ann … *(Fast pose.)* and because he has a thing for the real Ann, he follows me and I run to the *Foxy Felicia* theatre and we wait there for you so you can put the big monkey in your show instead of Dennam's show!

MYRON. Beautiful! You got it! *(Stands.)*

DAISY. I got it! And then … !

MYRON. Good! *(Beat.)* And then?

DAISY. And then you get your writer to write up a juicy part for me in *Foxy Felicia*!

MYRON *(beat)*. Did I say I'd do that?

DAISY. Nope. I did! Ain't that a great idea?

MYRON. Uh … Well, Daisy … I don't think your mother …

DAISY. Because you know what, Uncle Myron?

MYRON. What?

DAISY. If you don't get me that part, I ain't seducin' your monkey!

SALLY. She's in town three hours, she already knows how to play the game.

DAISY. I'm from Buffalo. I ain't from Mars.

(The main door flies open, and WILLIE rushes in.)

WILLIE. Boss!

MYRON. Willie! Did you find Jack?

WILLIE. No! But I found the dame!

MYRON. Ann?

WILLIE. Yes!

MYRON. Great!

WILLIE. No!

MYRON. What?

WILLIE. I lost her!

MYRON. Ann?

WILLIE. Yes!

SALLY *(in disgust)*. Great!

MYRON. No!

DAISY. What?

WILLIE. When I got to the theatre, she was runnin' out, and Mrs. S. was chasin' her! Ann was shakin' a piece of paper in Mrs. S's face, then Mrs. S. grabbed for her, but Ann run away up 32nd!

MYRON. Did you follow her?

WILLIE. I tried, but I lost her in a pack a' nuns.

MYRON. Nuns!

WILLIE. Yeah! They was comin' around 8th Avenue and I slammed into about six of 'em. Cut my finger on one of their … wing spans. *(Illustrates the wing span.)* Two of 'em called me things I didn't know nuns knew!

MYRON. So where is Ann now?

WILLIE. I don't know!

(WILLIE sits beside DAISY on the sofa. The doorbell rings.)

SALLY. Maybe that's her!

MYRON *(runs to door)*. How can that be her? What do you think this is, some kind of farce?

(MYRON opens the door. ANN is standing there.)

ANN. Where is Jack?

MYRON. Jack?

SALLY *(loud whisper)*. Willie!

(SALLY indicates that WILLIE should hide DAISY as they sit on the sofa. He does. With his hat. She slinks down on the sofa under the hat.)

ANN *(entering)*. Yes, Jack! He sent me this note. *(Slaps it to MYRON.)*

MYRON *(reads)*. "Ann. Get out of that theatre as fast as you can and come back to the hotel room. I could be already dead which might affect our marriage. Hurry. Your loving lover, Jack Driskel." *(To ANN.)* You came back here on your own? You're not afraid of Dennam?

ANN. I came back for Jack. Jack saved me from the dinosaurs. It's the least I could do.

SALLY. I'm still havin' trouble with the dinosaurs …

MYRON *(grabs ANN)*. Come on!

ANN. Where is Jack!

MYRON *(as he ushers ANN towards DAISY's room)*. Uh … he's … in this room, here! He's been waitin' for ya!

(MYRON opens the door for ANN. She steps in, looks inside and holds the door open.)

ANN. This room is empty!

MYRON. It ain't now!

(MYRON shoves ANN into the room and slams the door shut, locking it. DAISY emerges from behind WILLIE on the sofa and stares moonily at him.)

MYRON *(cont'd)*. Great! Now! We still got time! Daisy! I want you to sit next to the phone in that bedroom … *(Indicates BERTRILLE's room.)* As soon as I know the coast is clear, I'll call you, you come meet me at the Alhambra!

SALLY. What's wrong with this phone?

MYRON. I need her to concentrate. *(Indicates moony DAISY and WILLIE.)* She gets distracted.

DAISY. Can you blame me?

WILLIE. Can you blame her?

MYRON *(points)*. In there. Wait till I call.

DAISY. Roger! *(Heads to the room. At the door.)* And out! Ha! *(Enters the room and slams the door.)*

WILLIE. Uh, Boss … I been thinkin' … Ain't it a little dangerous for Daisy makin' like she's the real Ann?

SALLY. Yeah, Myron.

WILLIE. I mean, we ain't seen this monkey, yet, and …

MYRON. Don't worry about Daisy. She's got Siegel blood in her!

WILLIE. That's my point.

MYRON. Never mind! You're gonna find Bertrille and keep her outa my way!

SALLY. What about me?

MYRON *(tosses room key to SALLY)*. You make sure the voyager stays in that room! And if Jack shows up, send him to me at the Alhambra!

SALLY. But I'm supposed to meet Higginbottom at the Regency!

MYRON. I'll get a message to him, tell him you'll be a little late. I don't want him to know anything about this. I just want him to think everything is peachy keen. *(Moves to the main door.)*

SALLY. But, Myron, he'll be expecting …

MYRON *(opens the door)*. To hell with Higginbottom!

(And there stands HIGGINBOTTOM.)

HIGGINBOTTOM. To vhere vid who?

MYRON. Uh … it's a new … American … expression of … respect! Yes! Right, everybody? Yes! "To hell with Higginbottom!"

MYRON, SALLY & WILLIE. To hell with Higginbottom!

HIGGINBOTTOM *(beat)*. Vell … tank you … to hell vid you, too … But you should probably know dat … *(Shows boat ticket.)*

MYRON. No time, Sig. No time. Come on, Willie, we have work to do! *(Ushers WILLIE out the door.)*

HIGGINBOTTOM. But da szhow, she is … *(Raspberry.)* I am taking my checkbook and going back to Budapest!

MYRON *(at door)*. Sig … you promised to give me till midnight, now, didn't you?

HIGGINBOTTOM. Midnight, schmidnight! I zee *Felicia*, von last time, den I go! *(Starts rummaging through his pockets.)* I hef got my tickets for da boat! I am tru vid da schow biznezz! *(Keeps rummaging.)*

MYRON *(with meaning)*. Ma! Take care of this!

SALLY. Whatdya mean?

MYRON. Whatdya think I mean? *(More deep meaning.)* Take care of this. Entertain the man!

SALLY *(gets it)*. Oh, Jesus, no.

MYRON *(under his breath, again demonstrating)*. "Boomp-boomp-pa-boomp … !"

SALLY. Oh, Jesus, no.

MYRON. Bye! *(Leaves, slamming the door, of course.)*

HIGGINBOTTOM *(finds tickets)*. Aha! Zally … da schow! Vee go!

SALLY *(as cheerily as she can get)*. Sig! Wait! I thought you were going to meet me in the lobby.

HIGGINBOTTOM *(shows ticket)*. Dey vere fast vid de boat ticket, so I come to meet you here. Come! To da schow!

SALLY. Uh … uh … wait! Let me get you a drink! *(Goes to the bar.)*

HIGGINBOTTOM *(intercepts her and brings her to the door)*. No. No drink! Must get zip zip to da theatre! Almost time for da curtains. Vee been vid da shilly shally all da time vid da monkey and da mongoose man and da cheneral hoo hoo. I vant to zee my *Felicia* von last time and den …

(He opens the main door and is about to shove SALLY through it. She stops him and stands firm.)

SALLY. No! Sig! I absolutely insist you stay for a drink!

(A loud banging begins to sound on the other side of the door where ANN is being held captive.)

SALLY *(cont'd)*. OK, Sig, you win. Let's go. *(Starts out.)*

HIGGINBOTTOM *(stops)*. Vait! Vhat iss vid diss banging?

SALLY. What banging?

HIGGINBOTTOM. On da door dere. Dere iss banging on da door comink from da inside!

SALLY. I don't hear a thing.

(The banging gets louder and more intense.)

HIGGINBOTTOM. Dere! Dere! Boom, boom. Bang, bang. You hear dat?

ANN *(from offstage)*. Help! I'm being held captive!

HIGGINBOTTOM. Vhat? *(To SALLY.)* Who hef you captivated?

(He moves toward ANN's door. SALLY makes a beeline for the door and beats him to it, blocking his way. She is wailing as she moves.)

SALLY. NOOOOO! *(She is there.)* You can't open this door!

HIGGINBOTTOM *(moves)*. Yes, I can. Vatch.

SALLY *(stops him)*. No! That's my granddaughter! Daisy! She's … under quarantine!

HIGGINBOTTOM. For vhat?

SALLY. For … leprosy!

HIGGINBOTTOM. Vhat!

(The doorbell rings.)

HIGGINBOTTOM *(cont'd)*. First da bang bang, now da ding-dong.

(He heads for the main door. Once again, SALLY, wailing all the way, beats him to it and blocks it.)

SALLY. NOOOOOO! *(Again, she's there first.)* Sig … Sig … I gotta be honest with you.

HIGGINBOTTOM. You gotta?

(ANN is still banging, and the doorbell is still ringing. All timed with the joke lines, of course!)

SALLY. I gotta … Sig … *(Bites the bullet.)* Oh, Jesus … Sig … *(Struggles.)* I want you.

HIGGINBOTTOM. You do?

SALLY. I do.

HIGGINBOTTOM. Vhat … do you … vant me … for?

SALLY *(aside)*. I'm asking myself the same question! *(Escorts him to her bedroom door.)* Wait … for me … here … in my … bedroom! I'll be … right in and we'll … we'll …

HIGGINBOTTOM *(confused)*. Ooh … *(Gets it.)* OOOH! You vant da schtoop!

SALLY. Yes! Yes! Da schtoop. Gimme da schtoop!

HIGGINBOTTOM. Vell, now! Dat does call for da schnapps! *(Heads to the bar.)*

SALLY *(stops him, leads him to room)*. No! Now! I want you NOW! Wait in there!

(She shoves HIGGINBOTTOM into the room and slams the door. The doorbell rings. SALLY starts for door. Instantly, there is loud banging coming from ANN in DAISY's room.)

ANN *(from room)*. Let me out of here!!!

SALLY. All right, honey, you asked for it!

(SALLY unlocks DAISY's door and opens it. ANN sticks her head out. SALLY grabs her by the scruff of the neck and makes a fist.)

ANN. You wouldn't dare! I am a lady!

SALLY. Yeah? Well, I'm a stripper!

(SALLY slugs ANN. "Oof!" ANN falls back into the room. SALLY slams the door, locks it and turns back into the room, slapping her hands together as if just completing a successful boxing match. The doorbell keeps ringing. SALLY, stopping a second to huff and puff, heads to the main door and opens it. JACK stands there.)

JACK *(bounds into the room)*. Is she here?

SALLY. Who?

JACK *(stepping inside)*. Ann! I left a note in her dressing room. Then I had to go feed the attraction. When I got back, the note was gone and so was she!

SALLY *(shoving him back to door)*. She's here, Jack! She's safe. Now—Myron wants you back at the Alhambra! Pronto!

JACK. But if I go back there without Ann, Dennam'll have my hide!

SALLY *(still shoving him to door)*. Myron has it all figured out. Just get your hide over to the theatre and find Myron!

JACK. Where is she? *(Breaks away and heads to ANN's room.)* She in here?

(And, yes, one more time, SALLY wails and beats him to the door.)

SALLY. NOOOOOO! *(She's there.)* She's … sleeping!

JACK. Sleeping?

SALLY. Out cold.

JACK. Oh. Well … poor kid. She's had a rough day. She's been manipulated, you know. Besides … I suppose she's gonna need her strength for tomorrow night.

SALLY *(yanks him towards door)*. Yeah. Yeah. Strength. *(Stops.)* What?

JACK. We're gettin' … married. *(With meaning.)* You know … married?

SALLY *(continues to door)*. Oh. Right. Married.

JACK. She's gonna need her rest.

SALLY *(they reach door)*. No doubt. Now get to the theatre and Myron will tell you what to do!

JACK. How much time before the show?

SALLY. Less than an hour! Go! Go! Go! *(Still pushing.)*

JACK *(halfway out door, irritated)*. You know, you people over here yell and scream and talk so fast it don't give a fella a minute to think!

SALLY *(stops pushing)*. All right. All right. You want a minute to think? Fine. Good. Go ahead. Think.

(JACK bears down and tries to think. He tries really hard.)

SALLY *(cont'd)*. Anything comin'?

JACK. 'Fraid not.

SALLY. That's a shame.

JACK. I'm used to it.

SALLY. Get to the theatre!

(And she shoves him out the door, slamming it. As soon as she closes the door, HIGGINBOTTOM's door opens. He stands there now in classic hideous boxer shorts, with garters, and silly T-shirt.)

HIGGINBOTTOM *(cheerfully)*. Ready!

(SALLY drops her head to her chest, walks to the bar, grabs a bottle and heads to the bedroom.)

HIGGINBOTTOM *(cont'd)*. I should probably warn you—in Budapest, I am considered quite a man of da ladies!

SALLY. Is that right?

HIGGINBOTTOM *(gleefully)*. Brace yourself!

(SALLY continues reluctantly to bedroom. The telephone rings.)

SALLY *(to the heavens)*. Thank you, God! *(To HIGGINBOTTOM.)* I'll be right in.

HIGGINBOTTOM *(meaningfully, subtly indicating)*. But I'm ready now!

SALLY *(going to the phone)*. Hang on to it! Think about Joan Blondell!

HIGGINBOTTOM *(questioning)*. Joan Blondell? *(Takes a look, beat.)* Ooo! It vorks!

(He turns, smiles and re-enters the bedroom, shutting the door. SALLY answers the phone.)

SALLY. Hello! … Myron! … Yes! Don't worry about Higginbottom! Listen! Jack was just here! I sent him over to you … What? … Oh, Ann is fine … No, I don't have to check … I gave her a sedative … *(Shows her fist.)* You want me to send Daisy over? … Well, hurry up, she's waiting in the other room for your call! …

HIGGINBOTTOM *(opens the door and sticks head out. Happily, sing-song).* Oh, Joan! Ziggy is vaiting!

SALLY *(pained).* Myron, I gotta go. I'm making the ultimate sacrifice! … What? … No! I only wish I could kill myself!

HIGGINBOTTOM *(appears fully again. Amorously, singsong).* Hel-looooo!

SALLY *(into the phone).* Get that monkey!

(She hangs up and heads to HIGGINBOTTOM's door. HIGGINBOTTOM offers a little growl.)

SALLY *(cont'd).* GET BACK IN THERE!

HIGGINBOTTOM. Oo! I like it vit da yellink!

SALLY. And hold onto that pigeon!

(SALLY shoves him into the room and slams the door shut. As she does, the main door opens and BERTRILLE sticks her head inside.)

BERTRILLE. Nobody's here!

(She enters, followed by DENNAM.)

DENNAM. Is Ann here?

BERTRILLE. What, I'm not speaking American? THERE'S NOBODY HERE! *(Starts rummaging around the fruit.)* They must have gone to *Foxy Felicia.*

DENNAM. What are you looking for?

BERTRILLE. That paper I told you about!

DENNAM *(dismissive)*. Ah, it couldn't have been what you thought it was. Dad said Siegel didn't have a copy.

BERTRILLE. Well, I saw a copy! That … Daisy kid had it!

DENNAM. Forget about the paper, will ya! By midnight tonight, it'll be too late for Siegel to do anything about it. And tomorrow, when we're the hit of the world, you and me, we take that showbiz lovin' little niece of his out to lunch, throw a few hundred bucks in her pocketbook, set her up in a nice apartment, get her an agent … presto! She gives that little piece of paper to us, and before you know it, I'm king of Broadway! *(Goes to the phone.)* Maybe she went back to the theatre!

BERTRILLE. Why didn't you lock her in the dressing room like I told you?

DENNAM *(taps the bar for the operator. Into the phone)*. Get me the Alhambra!

BERTRILLE *(shows note)*. That's where she found this note from "Jack." Who's Jack?

DENNAM *(to BERTRILLE)*. The first mate on the ship. Her boyfriend. *(Into the phone.)* AL-HAM-BRA! AL as in AL. HAM as in HAM. BRA as in … ALHAMBRA!

BERTRILLE. Ann's not at the theatre, Dennam! She's run out on you! *(Sits on the sofa.)*

DENNAM. She didn't run out on me!

BERTRILLE. How do you know?

DENNAM. She's a woman!

(As he holds the receiver, the other telephone rings in the bedroom.)

DENNAM *(cont'd)*. What's that?

BERTRILLE. The telephone!

DENNAM *(the phone in his hand)*. Then what's this?

BERTRILLE. In the other room, genius! Listen! *(Listens.)* One ring! Somebody picked up!

DENNAM. Maybe Ann's still here! Get those lights!

(He hangs up the phone. BERTRILLE flicks off the main lights. She and DENNAM hide in the shadows. DAISY emerges from the bedroom, still dressed like ANN, with the blonde wig. She moves to the door then stops and fidgets uncomfortably for a second.)

DAISY *(stops)*. Oops. Better go now. *(Heads for the bathroom.)* Won't get a chance once the monkey starts chasin' me!

(She enters the bathroom and closes the door. DENNAM and BERTRILLE emerge and whisper.)

DENNAM. That's Ann.

BERTRILLE. Yes.

DENNAM *(to BERTRILLE)*. Is that the can?

BERTRILLE. Yes.

DENNAM. So. Ann's in the can.

BERTRILLE *(moves to the bathroom)*. Let's get her!

DENNAM *(stops her)*. Wait! She'll come out on her own!

BERTRILLE. How do you know?

DENNAM *(beat)*. It's the can!

BERTRILLE. Then we'll grab her!

DENNAM. No! She don't react good to the rough stuff. She ain't like you.

BERTRILLE. Whatdya mean by that?

DENNAM *(meaningfully)*. You know what I mean.

BERTRILLE *(beat, eyeballs him)*. Yes. I do.

(From SALLY's room comes HIGGINBOTTOM's voice.)

HIGGINBOTTOM *(offstage, whining).* "No! No! No!"

(This time they hide behind the sofa. SALLY's bedroom door opens and HIGGINBOTTOM appears. He has one of SALLY's very flowing and feminine robes wrapped around him.)

HIGGINBOTTOM. It chust vorks bedda vhen I use da wasoline! Be holting your horses!!

(He heads to the bathroom. He opens the door. Before he can see who's in there, DAISY shrieks! And then HIGGINBOTTOM shrieks! As he does, the robe falls off, and he is in his full underwear glory. DAISY slams the bathroom door closed. HIGGINBOTTOM races away squealing. Perhaps he leaps over the sofa, stepping on the cushions, and heads back to SALLY's bedroom, where he enters and slams the door. DENNAM and BERTRILLE's heads pop up from behind the sofa.)

DENNAM. Who the hell was that?

BERTRILLE. Higginbottom! Myron's money man!

DENNAM. What's he doin' here?

BERTRILLE. Looks like he's making a deposit!

(The bathroom door opens. They duck behind the sofa again. DAISY sticks her head out of the bathroom, carefully.)

DAISY. Hello? *(Steps out into room.)* Are you gone, scary underwear man?

(She's convinced the coast is clear. She steps out of the bathroom, sees the robe on the floor and picks it up. She moves carefully toward the sofa, where she plans to put the robe. DENNAM steps out from the shadows, approaches her from behind. He speaks before she can get to the sofa.)

DENNAM. Hey!

DAISY *(freezes, does not look back)*. I'm an actress! Not a prostitute!

DENNAM *(holds her by the waist from behind)*. Don't I know that, baby? You're the actress that's gonna make my monkey happy tonight!

DAISY. I never heard it called that before.

DENNAM. Oh, that's right. I forgot. I broke my own rule. I should have called it … my attraction.

DAISY. Well, ain't you a mugger with high self esteem.

DENNAM. Without you, my attraction just lies there, peelin' bananas …

DAISY. Now, there's somethin' that'd sell tickets.

(The main door opens. WILLIE enters and turns on the lights. He sees DENNAM holding DAISY.)

WILLIE. Hey!

(WILLIE whips out his gun and leaps for DENNAM.

DENNAM pulls DAISY away and dodges WILLIE.

WILLIE trips and falls over the sofa. As he does, his gun fires, which breaks the doorknob on DAISY's door where ANN is locked inside.

DAISY screams and runs to WILLIE.

DENNAM chases her to WILLIE and grabs for her.

She screams again and runs around the sofa, heading towards her bedroom door.

WILLIE intercepts DENNAM and starts grappling with him on the floor.

ANN has emerged from the room. She and DAISY meet, do the "ET" thing, scream, and ANN chases DAISY out the main door.

DENNAM is grappling with WILLIE on the floor. BER-TRILLE has been cowering behind the opened main door.

DENNAM finds SALLY's robe on the floor, throws it over WILLIE's head and emerges from the grapple. He looks around. He sees ANN exiting and races at her to the main door. He has not seen the two "Ann's" together.)

DENNAM. Ann! Ann!

(DENNAM exits the main door, following ANN. BER-TRILLE has been watching this.)

BERTRILLE. Hey! That's my dress! *(Heads to the door.)*

(WILLIE throws off the robe, rises and sees BERTRILLE going to the main door. He stops her.)

WILLIE. Oh, no, you don't!

(WILLIE drags BERTRILLE back into the room. She is kicking and screaming. SALLY and HIGGINBOTTOM emerge from the bedroom.)

SALLY. What the hell is going on out here?

WILLIE *(seeing HIGGINBOTTOM in his underwear)*. What the hell is going on in there?

SALLY *(looks at HIGGINBOTTOM's hoo-hoo)*. Not much.

(Having no words for what SALLY describes, HIGGIN-BOTTOM shrugs his shoulders and waves his hand in disgust at "hoo-hoo" height and gives a drooping raspberry.)

BERTRILLE. Sally! Tell this Neanderthal to release me!

WILLIE. Hey! I'm an American!

SALLY. You ain't goin' nowhere, floozie!

HIGGINBOTTOM. Oh! Dat's the floozie!

BERTRILLE. Well, I never …

WILLIE. That's not what I heard!

SALLY *(to BERTRILLE)*. SIDDOWN!

(WILLIE thrusts BERTRILLE into a chair)

SALLY *(cont'd)*. You've taken your last nickel from Myron! After tonight, my Myron will make chumps outa you and Dennam and everybody else on Broadway who's stepped on him all these years! My Myron is finally gonna sit on top of the world, lookin' down at the rest of you lowlifes. He'll have the finest food, the finest wine, the finest women! After tonight, my Myron is gonna be toast of the town! Man of the year! The real king of Broadway! I believe in my boy! I love him like a son! He'll make it! I know he will! All he has to do is get that monkey!

WILLIE. And if he don't?

SALLY. I'll kill him!

(Blackout. Music.)

SCENE 2

(In the blackout we hear the roar of an enormous gorilla. Out of the roar, we hear sounds of the Manhattan streets in chaos—horns blaring, sirens wailing, people screaming. Out of that [as that all continues in the background], we hear the voice of WINCHELL again, broadcasting.)

WINCHELL *(in breathless distress)*. Mr. and Mrs. America and all the ships at sea … this is Walter Winchell again, broadcasting from the Alhambra Theatre where only minutes ago, Carl Dennam's king sized gorilla named Kong ripped off his shackles and burst through the back wall of the theatre onto the Manhattan streets! The cheeky chimp appeared to be upset when the young actress Ann Farrow, who inexplicably kept adjusting her hair, stepped in front of the flashing cameras, followed by an Ann Farrow impersonator, who ran onstage and tackled the original Ann Farrow to the stage floor. After some heated but very entertaining biting and scratching, blonde and sultry Ann Farrow broke free from her blonde and sultry impersonator, eyeballed the monkey and ran out of the theatre screaming, "Here, Kong! Come and get it!"

(Lights up on the suite.

HIGGINBOTTOM, still trouserless, is pacing behind the sofa, mumbling in Hungarian, playing with a yo-yo [it's therapy].

WILLIE sits on the arm of the sofa, aiming his pistol at BER-TRILLE, who is tied up and gagged, sitting in a straight-back chair, steaming, occasionally mumbling inarticulate pleas to be released.

SALLY is at the radio, listening intently.)

WINCHELL *(cont'd).* Producer Carl Dennam tried desperately to maintain some decorum, but rival producer Myron Siegel leaped to the stage touting his own new show *Foxy Felicia* as the monkey ransacked the back wall like some drunken character in a Eugene O'Neill play.

SALLY. Good for you, Myron!

WINCHELL. Dennam and Siegel then engaged in a fist fight which ended abruptly when Siegel pulled down Dennam's pants!

WILLIE *(delighted).* Hey! Nice move, boss! *(To BERTRILLE.)* I taught him that! *(BETRILLE growls.)* Hey!

WINCHELL. Dennam ran out of the theatre after Siegel. Jack Driskel, the fiancée of at least one of the sultry blondes, then ran offstage hollering to anyone who would listen that he was, and I quote, "Going to get my rattlin' gun!"

(The sounds of the street take over for a second.)

SALLY *(to WILLIE)*. What's a rattlin' gun?

WILLIE *(shrugs)*. I'm oblivious.

> *(BERTRILLE, still gagged, mumbles, "No shit!" through the gag.)*

WINCHELL. Ladies and gentlemen, I thought I'd seen it all, but this takes the cake! A broadway audience has left the theatre before intermission without asking for money back, Carl Dennam has lost his trousers to Myron Siegel, and a 40-foot gorilla is chasing two slim and sultry blondes through the streets of New York!

> *(The sound of a Tommy gun is heard.)*

WINCHELL *(cont'd)*. And that must be the rattlin' gun! I gotta get outta here! This is Walter Winchell signing off for Shamrock Cigarettes! "It's worth the hack, so buy a pack!" Run for your lives!

> *(We hear the Shamrock Cigarettes jingle as SALLY clicks off the radio.)*

SALLY. Jesus Christ! *(Runs to the window.)*

HIGGINBOTTOM. I vill need pents! *(Runs to the bedroom.)*

> *(BERTRILLE is livid. She is making as much noise as she can through the gag, begging to be released. She is so energized, she is lifting the chair up from the floor and down again.)*

WILLIE. Mrs. S! You gotta be … you know … more … san-guine! *(BERTRILLE stops a second, in disbelief.)* That means you gotta …

(BERTRILLE reacts by becoming louder and even less sanguine. Her chair jumps up and down.)

WILLIE *(cont'd)*. All right, all right!!! *(Yanks the gag off BERTRILLE's mouth.)*

BERTRILLE. When I tell Dennam about this, you will wish for death, dictionary man!

SALLY *(looks out the window)*. Trust me, Dennam's problems are a lot bigger and hairier than anything in this room!

(HIGGINBOTTOM re-enters, fully pantsed. SALLY refers to him.)

SALLY *(cont'd)*. Except maybe him. *(Indicates the room where ANN was kept.)* I can't believe Ann got past us!

(Gorilla roar! SALLY looks out the window again and points.)

SALLY *(cont'd)*. Mother Machree in the mornin', look at that thing!

BERTRILLE. Untie me, you idiots!

WILLIE *(runs to the window)*. And there's Daisy with the other dame chasing her!

HIGGINBOTTOM. Daisy?

SALLY. And Kong is after both of them!

WILLIE. I gotta get down there and rescue her! *(Races to the main door.)*

HIGGINBOTTOM. I tot Daisy vass … *(Indicates bedroom.)*

BERTRILLE *(screams as WILLIE passes)*. You're a snack! That's all you are! A snack for that monkey!

(WILLIE exits, slamming the door.)

SALLY *(looking out window)*. Look at him! He's so confused!

HIGGINBOTTOM. Da monkey iss confuzed?

SALLY. Sexually.

HIGGINBOTTOM. Oh. Zexually. *(Beat.)* Vhat?

SALLY. He doesn't know which blonde he has a thing for! *(Opens the window.)*

HIGGINBOTTOM. Da monkey hass a ting?

SALLY *(leans out the window)*. DAISY! RUN LIKE HELL!

BERTRILLE. Sally!

SALLY. Shut up! It's because of you Ann escaped from the room here in the first place!

HIGGINBOTTOM. Vait a minnid! I taught Daisy vass in da room here!

SALLY *(looking out window)*. She was.

HIGGINBOTTOM. So iff da girl in da room here vas Daisy, how can she be chazing Daisy?

SALLY. The girl in the room was Ann!

HIGGINBOTTOM. So who iss Daisy?

SALLY. Daisy is supposed to be Ann.

HIGGINBOTTOM. Zo Ann iss Daisy?

SALLY. No. Ann is Ann.

HIGGINBOTTOM. I tot Daisy vass Ann.

SALLY. She is.

HIGGINBOTTOM. So Daisy iss Ann but Ann iss not Daisy?

SALLY. Bingo!

HIGGINBOTTOM. Ah! Who iss Bingo?

SALLY. Let me explain somethin' to you. Shut up!

BERTRILLE. Sally! Untie me! I'll cut you in on my piece of the monkey!

SALLY *(to BERTRILLE)*. Your piece of the monkey! Are you kidding! The only way you get a piece of that monkey is if you follow him down the street with a shovel.

(Enormous gorilla roar!)

SALLY *(cont'd)*. A great BIG shovel!

(The main door flies open, and DAISY runs in, out of breath.)

DAISY. Is she here?

SALLY. Daisy! Thank God! Is who here?

DAISY. Ann! I lost her in the Automat. I grabbed a big slice
of pie from a boy scout and threw it at her. She was blinded
by the meringue. I made the boy scout cry, but I got away.
She's nuts! *(To BERTRILLE.)* Hi, Tushie! Boy, was I ever
wrong about Ann bein' you!

BERTRILLE *(calmly)*. Can you untie me, please?

SALLY. NO!

(BERTRILLE screams.)

HIGGINBOTTOM *(at window)*. I tink …

DAISY. Where's Willie?

HIGGINBOTTOM. I tink da monkey …

SALLY. He ran outta here a second ago, looking for you.

DAISY. Out there!? With Kong!? No! He's too delicate!
(Runs towards the main door.)

HIGGINBOTTOM *(sing-song)*. I tink da monkey iss coming
dis vay …

(DAISY opens the door, looks out and stops in her tracks.)

DAISY. SHIT! *(Slams the door closed.)* It's her! *(Runs to the
bathroom.)* Keep her away from me! *(Opens the door, enters
and stops.)* She has jungle training! *(Slams the door closed.)*

*(The main door opens. ANN enters. Her face is obliterated
with pie. She slams the door shut.)*

ANN. Where's the bitch!?

(SALLY and HIGGINBOTTOM point at BERTRILLE.)

ANN *(cont'd)*. Not that bitch! The young bitch!
BERTRILLE. Well, I never … !
ANN. That's not what I heard!

> *(The main door opens. WILLIE enters. Sees ANN. Her face is camouflaged.)*

WILLIE. Daisy! What're you runnin'! I was scared for ya!

> *(He grabs ANN, plants a huge smooch on her face. DAISY, having heard WILLIE's voice, comes out of the bathroom. ANN breaks away from WILLIE. His face is now covered with pie.)*

ANN. How dare you!

> *(ANN slaps WILLIE in the face. DAISY has stepped behind ANN. She turns ANN around.)*

DAISY. How dare YOU!

> *(She slaps ANN in the face. ANN screams and yanks DAISY to the floor, where a battle ensues, again with biting and scratching, again very entertaining. WILLIE tries to separate them but falls all over himself. DAISY finally breaks away and hides behind HIGGINBOTTOM at the window. WILLIE grabs ANN and holds her back.)*

DAISY *(cont'd)*. It ain't my fault your monkey likes me better!
HIGGINBOTTOM. Da monkey hass a ting, you know.

> *(ANN kicks WILLIE in a sensitive area. He howls in pain and falls to the sofa. ANN rushes at DAISY. DAISY gets away and runs around the sofa. ANN chases DAISY. SALLY goes to see if WILLIE is all right.)*

DAISY *(roaring at WILLIE, pointing)*. DOOR! *(Runs once around the sofa.)* WILLIE!

(As DAISY passes around again, SALLY joins in, running behind DAISY and ahead of ANN. WILLIE, still in pain but getting the idea, rises, hobbles up to and opens the door. DAISY runs inside. ANN follows her. Screaming. In a second, DAISY emerges from the room.)

DAISY *(cont'd, again roaring)*. DOOR!

(WILLIE slams the door closed.)

DAISY *(cont'd, breathless, to SALLY)*. KEY!
SALLY. Key!

(SALLY tosses the key to WILLIE, who locks the door. DAISY, now out of breath, begins to pant. SALLY is now panting. WILLIE pants. HIGGENBOTTOM looks at everybody else, then pants, although he's done nothing.)

SALLY *(cont'd, to DAISY)*. What happened at the theatre?

DAISY *(breathlessly)*. Everything was goin' according to Uncle Myron's plan. They opened the curtain. Kong was in his chains. Dennam introduced me to the audience. Even he couldn't tell the difference with all those stage lights in his eyes.

SALLY. What about Jack?

DAISY. Uncle Myron explained the whole plan to him.

SALLY. Good!

DAISY. He didn't understand a word of it. But there was no turnin' back! I walked onstage!

SALLY. So what went wrong?

DAISY. The flashbulbs! Kong went screwy! The monkey thought the flashbulbs were attacking me! And then when Ann showed up, his eyes bulged out like … like … *(There's a little ape in her imitation.)* "What the bejesus is goin' on here?" His gorilla hormones musta went all outa whack. He didn't know what the hell was happenin'!

(JACK comes through the main door. He has his rattlin' gun. It's a machine gun. He points the gun into the room. Everybody reaches for the sky. BERTRILLE, whose wrists are tied to the chair, can't reach. JACK points the gun directly at her. Instantly, she raises her hands as far as she can.)

JACK. Where's Ann?

DAISY *(tries to calm him)*. Look, Jack … you gotta try to …

JACK. I mean the real Ann! You … you … phony baloney!

WILLIE. Hey!

SALLY *(points to door)*. In there, Jack. Go calm her down. Tell her to get some sleep while we figure all this out.

JACK *(waving his Tommy gun wildly, everybody ducks)*. It's no use, lady. Kong has gone bonkers!

SALLY. Gimme that! *(Grabs his Tommy gun.)* Where did you get a thing like this?

JACK. Birthday present.

SALLY *(uses the gun to move JACK to ANN's door)*. Get in there! Get! Get! Get!

JACK *(enters bedroom with ANN, sticks head back out as SALLY tries to close door)*. Hey! *(SALLY stops.)* If Kong should come by …

SALLY. What!

JACK *(with the utmost sincerity)*. Don't let him in!

SALLY *(shoves him inside the bedroom)*. Get in there!

HIGGINBOTTOM *(at window)*. Da monkey! Da monkey!

SALLY. What about da monkey?

HIGGINBOTTOM. He iss climbing up da side of da hotel!

DAISY *(runs to the window)*. He's looking right up here!

SALLY *(runs to the window)*. What!?

WILLIE *(also runs to the window)*. Lemme look!

DAISY. Holy shit!

WILLIE *(admonishing)*. Daisy!

DAISY. It's OK, Willie! It's OK to say that here!

WILLIE. You sure?

DAISY. I'm sure!

WILLIE *(looks)*. Holy shit!

SALLY *(indicates BERTRILLE)*. Untie her! We may need help shoving him off the building!

(WILLIE unties BERTRILLE.)

HIGGINBOTTOM *(yells out the window like a grammar school principal)*. Down, monkey! Monkey! Get down!

SALLY. What're we gonna do?!

DAISY *(back to the window)*. Here he comes!

HIGGINBOTTOM. He iss reaching for da balcony!! Look out! *(Also runs away from the window.)*

SALLY. Run!

(BERTRILLE is now free. She, SALLY, DAISY and HIG-GINBOTTOM scream at the top of their lungs. They try to reach the main door but are caught in the crossfire when one humongous gorilla paw explodes into the room through the balcony door and grabs onto the wall. The impact of the paw's arrival knocks them to the floor. It is a mammoth moment of chaos. Kong roars. Everybody onstage screams some more. SALLY, HIGGINBOTTOM and BERTRILLE recover and start throwing fruit, throw pillows and sofa cushions at the throbbing paw. DAISY races back to the window and looks out. WILLIE pulls out his gun and aims.)

SALLY *(cont'd, stops him)*. No! We need him for the show!

DAISY. He's reaching for the other room!

SALLY. He wants Ann!

DAISY. Go get her, Kong!

HIGGINBOTTOM *(at the bedroom, trying to open the locked door)*. Mizz! Mizz Blondie! *(Starts banging on the door.)* You muzt be evacuatink! You muzt get out of dere! Da monkey vill eat you!

SALLY *(pulls HIGGINBOTTOM from the door)*. She can handle herself!

DAISY *(at window)*. Too late! His other paw is in the bedroom!

> *(MYRON bursts into the room from the main door. He's got a bloody nose and a black eye. He is carrying a very large bag of bananas. Yes. Bananas.)*

MYRON. The monkey's climbing up the building!

SALLY *(indicating the paw)*. Thank you, Mr. News Flash!

MYRON. I got bananas!

SALLY. Why?

MYRON *(heads toward the balcony)*. To get his mind off sex!

SALLY. What?!

MYRON. Always works for me!

> *(MYRON holds up a drooping banana. Then he goes to the balcony and starts throwing bananas out at Kong.)*

DAISY *(at the window)*. The paw's comin' outta the room!

> *(ANN screams offstage.)*

BERTRILLE. Myron! Look what you've done!

DAISY. He's got her!

MYRON *(referring to BERTRILLE)*. What's she doin' here?!

DAISY *(at the window)*. He's takin' her with him!!

MYRON *(points to the gorilla hand)*. Grab him!

HIGGINBOTTOM. Vhat!

MYRON. Don't let him get away!! Everybody grab hold!

(MYRON drops the bag of bananas. Everybody leaps for the paw, grabs onto it for dear life and tries to keep it in the room. Even BERTRILLE gets dragged into the mix. The gorilla growls in protest. DAISY watches out the window.)

MYRON *(cont'd)*. Hold on! He opens in *Felicia* tomorrow!

SALLY. We're losin' him!

(After a moment, BERTRILLE takes an opportunity to creep towards the main door.)

DAISY. Aw! Leave him alone! He's just a crazy kid in love!

SALLY *(sees BERTRILLE)*. Myron! Look!

MYRON *(leaves the paw)*. Hey! Where do you think you're goin'?!

(As MYRON breaks toward BERTRILLE, the paw wrenches away from the balcony, and SALLY and HIGGINBOTTOM fall ignominiously to the floor. MYRON cuts off BERTRILLE before she reaches the door and brings her back into the room. As this happens, DAISY's bedroom door bursts open and JACK emerges, holding a broken chair leg. He is in a daze.)

JACK. He hit me!

MYRON *(shoves BERTRILLE onto the chair and tosses rope to WILLIE)*. Willie!

(WILLIE reties her.)

JACK. I tried to beat him off with a chair, but he hit me!

MYRON. You tried to beat him off with a chair!

(DENNAM races in through the main door.)

DENNAM. Siegel!

BERTRILLE. Dennam!

MYRON. Haha! Where's your monkey now, Dennam!

DENNAM. I thought he got as far as this room!

BERTRILLE. Well, he left, sugar! He's climbing up to the roof with your chippie!

DENNAM. What?!

JACK. The roof! With Ann? *(Aside to BERTRILLE.)* Ann's the chippie, right?

BERTRILLE. Right.

JACK. I'm goin' up there! *(Rushes out the door.)*

DENNAM. I'll go with you!

BERTRILLE. Dennam! Don't you see that I'm tied up here!

DENNAM. You told me you liked that.

MYRON *(to BERTRILLE)*. You do?

BERTRILLE. Dennam!

DENNAM *(beat)*. Bye! *(Runs out the main door.)*

DAISY *(looking out the window)*. He's left the roof! He's jumped to another building!

SALLY. What do you think, impresario? You got any ideas?

MYRON *(goes to the phone and slaps the bar for the operator)*. You bet I do! *(Into the phone.)* The Regency Theatre! Pronto! *(To SALLY.)* If he likes one blonde, how do you think he'll feel about a whole chorus?

SALLY. What?

MYRON *(into the phone)*. Hello! Maxie! Siegel! Get me backstage! *(To SALLY.)* Thinks he's a big ladies' man, huh? I'll give him somethin' to think about! *(Into the phone.)* Larry! Siegel! I want you to stop the show!

HIGGINBOTTOM. Ztop *Felicia*?

MYRON *(into the phone)*. You heard me! Stop the show and send every blond chorus girl in the cast out on the street!

WILLIE. Boss!

MYRON *(into the phone)*. Yeah! And tell 'em I want 'em all to follow the big monkey!

SALLY. Not bad, Myron!

MYRON *(into the phone)*. I'll send another girl down with instructions!

HIGGINBOTTOM. Holy zshit!

MYRON *(into the phone)*. Don't ask questions, just do it! *(Hangs up and turns to DAISY.)* Daisy! I want you to go down to the Regency, meet the chorus line and take them to Kong! As soon as he picks up the scent, you and the girls lead him back to the Regency. Can you do that?

DAISY *(reluctant)*. But Uncle Myron …

MYRON. Hey! You wanna be in that show or don't you?

DAISY. Oh, shoot! Yes! More than anything in the world!

MYRON. Then get goin'! And whatever you do, don't stop till you know Kong has picked up the scent! Lead those blondes all the way to the monkey!

SALLY. All the way to the monkey!

DAISY. All the way to the monkey?

MYRON. All the way to the monkey!

DAISY *(starts and stops)*. But will the girls listen to me?

MYRON. They'd better!

SALLY *(gives DAISY JACK's Tommy gun)*. This'll help.

MYRON. Great! Now go!

DAISY *(goes to the door)*. Right! *(Stops.)* Can I ask one question?

MYRON. What?

DAISY. Why is Tushie tied up?

MYRON. Her name's not Tushie! That's your Aunt Bertrille!

DAISY. Oh, so she's …

MYRON. Yes!

DAISY. Been in cahoots with …

MYRON. Yes!

DAISY. So that when he took over *Felicia* …

MYRON. Yes!

DAISY. She could get into …

MYRON. YES!

DAISY. And HE could get into …

MYRON. YES! YES! YES!

DAISY *(goes to shake BERTRILLE's hand)*. I could learn a lot from you.

MYRON *(intercepting her)*. GET OUTTA HERE!

(DAISY runs to the door. SALLY runs to the window.)

MYRON *(cont'd, to DAISY)*. All the way to the monkey!

DAISY *(as she exits, wielding the gun)*. All the way to the monkey!

(DAISY goes out the door. HIGGINBOTTOM has found MYRON's binoculars and moves to the window.)

WILLIE. Boss! I can't take it anymore! *(Moves to the door.)*

MYRON. Where you goin'? I need you here!

WILLIE. I can't let Daisy face that monkey alone!

MYRON. What alone? I'm sendin' 25 chorus girls!

WILLIE. Boss! I think … I think …

MYRON. You think what?

WILLIE. I think … I'm … infatuated!

MYRON. She's from Buffalo!

WILLIE. She can get over that!

MYRON. Aw, get outta here!

(WILLIE races out the door.)

HIGGINBOTTOM *(at the window with the binoculars)*. Zally! Look!

SALLY *(runs to the window and looks)*. He's climbing up the Empire State Building!

MYRON *(runs to the window)*. What?!

HIGGINBOTTOM. He iss carrying da blonde up da side of the Hempire Ztate Building!

SALLY. How will Daisy get to him now?!

(MYRON runs to the phone and slaps the bar.)

MYRON *(into the phone)*. Regency Theatre!

HIGGINBOTTOM *(looking out the window, matter-of-factly)*. Hees a very good climber.

MYRON. Backstage!

SALLY. He's a monkey!

MYRON *(into the phone)*. Backstage! … Larry! I sent my niece over there, has she … GREAT! Tell her to lead the blondes straight over to the Empire State Building … Why? Because that's where the monkey is! … No, this isn't code! Just do what I tell ya!

(DENNAM comes in the main door with JACK.)

JACK. Hey! Where's that Willie guy goin'?

DENNAM. Never mind him! *(To MYRON.)* We got Kong!

BERTRILLE. Dennam! Untie me!

DENNAM. In a minute. Enjoy it a little longer.

BERTRILLE. DENNAM!

MYRON. Whatdya mean you got Kong? I got 25 chorus girls gonna get him hotter than he ever was in that jungle paradise of his!

DENNAM. Chorus girls! What a pansie! Tell 'em what I got, Jack!

JACK. Airplanes!

MYRON. Airplanes?

DENNAM. Airplanes! I've arranged with the cops to shoot gas bombs at him from airplanes once he reaches the top of the Empire State! We knock him out, he faints on the observation deck, we lure him down with a couple of bananas, tomorrow he's back onstage with bigger chains! I get my million dollars!

BERTRILLE. DENNAM!

DENNAM *(moves to her)*. All right, baby, all right!

MYRON. You got a lot of nerve, Dennam!

DENNAM *(unties BERTRILLE)*. Yeah, and you know what else I got? *(She is free.)* I got your wife! *(They embrace.)*

MYRON *(to BERTRILLE, dramatically bitter)*. How could you?

BERTRILLE. I'm giving Carl the opportunity to express himself through my art!

DENNAM *(as he brings BERTRILLE to the balcony, to SALLY)*. Get outta the way!

SALLY. Aw, go express yourself!

DENNAM *(at balcony)*. Just think, baby. Once we get Kong under control, there's no stoppin' us! The hell with Farrow! Her only talent's in her caboose. She's yesterday's news!

JACK. Hey! That's my fiancée's caboose you're talkin' about!

DENNAM. Shaddup! *(To BERTRILLE.)* I'll build an entire show around you and Kong, baby! We'll take the *Beauty and the Beast* story and make it into a musical!

MYRON. *Beauty and the Beast* as a musical? New York'll never buy something like that! It won't run a week!

DENNAM. It'll run years, I tell you, years! Look! There's the planes!

MYRON *(runs to the phone and slaps the bar)*. I gotta call the Regency!

JACK. I'm going over there to be with Ann! *(Leaves.)*

MYRON *(into the phone)*. Regency! Backstage!

DENNAM. Aw, he's a dope, anyway! They deserve each other! *(Looks out the balcony, to BERTRILLE.)* Ain't that a gorgeous sight, baby!

BERTRILLE. Gorgeous!

DENNAM. All them beautiful airplanes! What'll they think of next?

MYRON *(into the phone)*. Larry! What happened with the girls?

DENNAM *(yells)*. Go get 'em, flyboys!

MYRON. Great! *(Hangs up.)* Daisy led 'em to the Empire State Building. Just watch, Dennam. In a couple of minutes Kong'll pick up the scent from my chorus line and he'll be on his way to the Regency!

DENNAM *(looks out the balcony)*. Dream on, Siegel! The planes are startin' to fire!

HIGGINBOTTOM *(looks out the window)*. Ouch! I tot you said dey vass shooting vit da gass?

DENNAM. Hey! Them ain't gas bombs!

BERTRILLE. What?

DENNAM. Them're bullets! He's gettin' hit with bullets!

MYRON *(goes to the window)*. You said they were just gonna knock him out!

HIGGINBOTTOM. Poor monkey! Vid da bullets in da neck!

SALLY *(runs to the window)*. What about Ann?

HIGGINBOTTOM. He put her down! Look! Nussing in hiss paw!

DENNAM *(runs to the phone)*. Lemme at that phone! *(Slaps the bar.)*

MYRON *(goes to the balcony and yells)*. Stop! I'll call Actors' Equity!!!

DENNAM *(into the phone)*. Get me the police station!

BERTRILLE *(runs to DENNAM)*. Fix this, Dennam! You promised me!

DENNAM. Shaddap! *(Into the phone.)* The precinct around the corner, whatdya think?

HIGGINBOTTOM *(still at the window)*. Bang! Dey hit him again!

MYRON. Gas bombs, my ass!

BERTRILLE. Dennam!

DENNAM *(into the phone)*. This is Dennam! What are they doing up there! I told you gas bombs, not bullets! … What?! They ARE gas bombs?! *(Hangs up.)* What the hell is going on?!

SALLY. Look, he's totterin' on the edge!

HIGGINBOTTOM. I can't look!

MYRON *(at the balcony)*. He's goin' down!

DENNAM *(at the window)*. They can't do this!

SALLY. Boy, once he hits the pavement, BANG! Municipal swimming pool!

DENNAM. Gas bombs, my ass!

MYRON. I already said that!

DENNAM. I said it better!

BERTRILLE. Dennam!

HIGGINBOTTOM *(at the window with the binoculars, his head reflects Kong's descent, as does his inflection)*. Oooooooh … monkey, monkey, monkey, monkey, monkey, monkey, monkeeeeeeeeeeee …

(The distant sound of a mega-gorilla hitting pavement. With the sound of the boom, all onstage are thrust about an inch into the air and down, tottering a bit. HIGGINBOTTOM turns away from the window and punctuates things with a tender raspberry.)

HIGGINBOTTOM *(cont'd)*. He flew waaay out dere when he fell! I tink … oh, dear … *(Looks out.)* I tink he landed on …

DENNAM. What am I gonna tell the press? See what you done, Siegel?! Now we're both up the creek without a paddle! Why, I oughta …

MYRON. Wait! Wait! I got a paddle! I got a paddle! You lost your monkey, sure … but I got … I still got *Felicia*!

SALLY. That's right, Myron! We can re-open tomorrow, with no competition!

MYRON. You hear that, Sig! *Felicia* is gonna be a hit after all!

BERTRILLE *(moves to MYRON, takes his arm)*. Myron, darling!

HIGGINBOTTOM *(looking out the window)*. Vell …

MYRON *(breaks away from BERTRILLE)*. How do you like them apples, Dennam?!

HIGGINBOTTOM. Dere is one ting …

MYRON. My Big Life Moment comin' true!

SALLY. That's my boy!

HIGGINBOTTOM. Da monkey …

MYRON. Top of the world, Ma!

HIGGINBOTTOM. Da monkey …

SALLY. Top of the … *(Beat, to HIGGENBOTTOM.)* What about the monkey?

HIGGINBOTTOM *(steps back in from the window)*. Da monkey … fell on da theatre.

MYRON. What?! The Regency?!

(MYRON runs to the window as HIGGINBOTTOM provides an affirming raspberry.)

DENNAM. Ha! Well I may not have a monkey! But at least I got a theatre!

BERTRILLE *(runs back to DENNAM)*. Yes! Yeah! At least we have a theatre!

DENNAM. I'll have an even more spectacular show in there within the month! I gotta get back to that island. Kong's gotta have an oversized relative or two I could capture. *(To BERTRILLE.)* Hey! You come too! Maybe I'll find one that's your type!

BERTRILLE. What? You want to use me to attract apes?

SALLY. Apes. Producers. Six of one …

DENNAM. Yeah! We'll find a mature monkey this time. One that won't fly off the handle like Kong. You know, a nice big ape that's been around the block a couple of times …

BERTRILLE. Well …

SALLY *(whacks MYRON upside the head)*. Arnold R. Siegel lives!

(Instantly, WILLIE bursts through the main door in a dither.)

WILLIE. Is she here? Is she? Is she?

MYRON. Who?

WILLIE. Daisy!

SALLY. Daisy? What happened to Daisy?

WILLIE *(with great animation and drive)*. I don't know! I got to the Empire State and I run into all the dolls from the show. They said Daisy went into the building alone. They said she promised the boss she'd go ALL THE WAY TO THE MONKEY! So I go up to the observation deck, and I don't see Daisy no place, so I start to head back down but before I can get the door open, I feel somethin' grabbin' at my pants. I turn around and I got a gorilla finger holdin' on to me. I'm face to face with Kong! And he's mad at me! He thinks I'm after Ann! He's seethin'! He's holdin' me by the pants and he's startin' to lift me up. I can see what he's gonna do! He's gonna throw me off the side of the building!

MYRON. How do you know?

WILLIE. A jealous gorilla's got me by the pants on top of the Empire State Building?! What do think he's gonna do with me!

HIGGINBOTTOM *(whacks MYRON upside the head)*. Yeah! What do you tink!

SALLY. Then what happened?

WILLIE. Well, I'm sayin' my prayers. I hold my breath. Kong lifts me up. He throws his arm back to toss me, and then …

MYRON. And then?

WILLIE. He gets a bullet in the neck! Then another! Then another! He lets me go! I fall to the deck. The bullets keep flyin'. The monkey is hurt! He goes to the precipice …

HIGGINBOTTOM. The vhat?

WILLIE. The edge of the buildin'! Look it up! He gets hit again! He falls! I'm safe! I'm overcome with emotion. I pass out for a few seconds. I wake up and I run back here. I never find Daisy. So where'd the bullets come from?

MYRON. Had to be the airplanes! But that still don't explain the cops sayin' they were shootin' gas bombs!

(DAISY explodes into the room, still carrying the Tommy gun. She's a mess. But she's smiling. She also has the sash from her dress wrapped around her head as a protective bandana. This time, think Rambo.)

DAISY. They were gas bombs!

WILLIE & SALLY. Daisy!

DAISY. No girl from Buffalo is gonna let a big monkey toss her man off a building!

WILLIE. Baby!

(WILLIE runs to DAISY. They embrace.)

MYRON *(sits on the sofa)*. My niece shot my monkey?

DAISY. Sorry, Uncle Myron.

DENNAM. What a pathetic bunch of losers! *(To DAISY.)* Except you. I like the looks of you. How about lunch tomorrow?

DAISY. Lunch? Me?

WILLIE *(suspiciously)*. Hey …

DENNAM *(to DAISY)*. I'll call you. *(To BERTRILLE.)* Come on, baby, let's go find us a bigger monkey!

BERTRILLE. Yes! We'll find a bigger monkey and renew the lease and we'll run forever!

MYRON. Lease?

SALLY. Lease?

HIGGINBOTTOM. Leaze?

DENNAM *(rushes BERTRILLE toward door, under his breath)*. Ixnay on the ease-lay, baby. Ixnay on the ease-lay!

MYRON. What about the lease?

DAISY. Lease? Oh! You must mean the letter Ma wanted me to give you.

DENNAM. What letter?

DAISY *(goes to the vase, gets the envelope and reads)*. This one. It says … *(Holds it up.)* "The lease!" See?

MYRON. Gimme that! *(Reads the first of two pages.)* "Dear Myron. Dad gave this to me 25 years ago and told me to hold onto it until it expired and then give it to you.

SALLY. What!

MYRON *(reading)*. "He gave it to me because he was afraid Ma was going to kill him after what happened … "

SALLY. I did threaten that occasionally …

MYRON. "And he thought you would lose it in a crap game. Send Daisy back home immediately, or I will disown you. Much love, Louise."

SALLY *(grabs the other page, reads)*. It's a copy of the lease to the Alhambra! It runs out … at midnight tonight!

MYRON *(to SALLY)*. He didn't lose it! He just leased it for free!

SALLY. At midnight tonight … *(Reads.)* "When full control of the premises will revert to the owner … "

MYRON & SALLY *(both reading)*. "Arnold R. Siegel!"

SALLY. And family!

MYRON. We got the Alhambra!

(They celebrate joyously.)

HIGGINBOTTOM. Oooh! And more zeats dere, too!

MYRON. More seats, more fannies!

HIGGINBOTTOM. More moniez! *(With a pronounced English accent.)* Jolly good show!

DENNAM *(to BERTRILLE)*. You and your big mouth!

(SALLY sidles up between BERTRILLE and DENNAM, gesturing appropriately.)

SALLY *(looks at BERTRILLE)*. 'Twas beauty … *(Looks at DENNAM.)* killed the beast.

DENNAM *(beat)*. Hey! That's what I'll tell the press! *(He rushes to the door, opens it and turns back.)* Wait! Wait! The jungle … the show … the dames … the monkey … the Empire State Building … This might make a great movie! *(Beat.)* Nah.

(DENNAM exits, slamming the door behind him. BERTRILLE stands, contemplating her next move.)

MYRON. I did it, Ma! I had my Big Life Moment!

SALLY. I never doubted you for a minute!

MYRON. And don't you worry, Daisy! I'll keep my word! You'll have a great part in the show!

DAISY *(to WILLIE)*. Didja hear that sweetcakes?!

MYRON. A great part! You had any experience as a virgin?

DAISY *(extremely excited)*. Plenty! *(Dips WILLIE and kisses him full on the lips.)*

MYRON. I'll make you a star! Starting tomorrow night, *Foxy Felicia* takes Broadway by storm! *(Goes to the bar.)*

HIGGINBOTTOM. My *Felicia*!

BERTRILLE *(sidles sexily up to HIGGINBOTTOM)*. Your *Felicia*?

HIGGINBOTTOM. Hmm? *(Perplexed, but interested.)* Oh!

BERTRILLE *(plays with hairpiece)*. Higgie Wiggie!

SALLY *(refers to BERTRILLE)*. Right back on the horse.

MYRON *(has made drinks for himself and SALLY and hands her one)*. I can't believe it. After everything we've been through … finally it's all over.

(Instantly, JACK tears in through the front door, greatly agitated.)

JACK. She here?

MYRON. Who?

JACK. Ann! I chased her all the way from the Empire State! I caught her at the lobby door and tried to hold her back, but she got away and said she'd get up here no matter how she done it! *(To DAISY.)* She wants your hide!

WILLIE *(protectively)*. It ain't her hide to have!

JACK. Tell that to Ann! She's as bonkers as Kong!

MYRON. So she's outside the building?

JACK. Yeah! I told the doorman to keep her out!

MYRON. So there's no way for her to get up here!

JACK. Right!

MYRON. Right. Good.

SALLY. Unless …

MYRON. Unless …

(As one, everybody slowly turns toward the French doors … there is a beat … then JACK speaks.)

JACK. Well … she does have the experience.

(The French doors burst open, and ANN stands there, completely disheveled, wild-eyed, looney. She screams and lunges for DAISY, who screams and runs away. ANN chases her. Music.

JACK and WILLIE make an attempt to keep the girls apart, but it's a lost cause and mayhem ensues. JACK and WILLIE prepare to box, feinting swipes. BERTRILLE grabs HIGGINBOTTOM's wig and teases him as he runs after her, trying to get it back from her.

The lights fade to feature MYRON and SALLY, standing solidly. They toast to each other.)

SALLY. Myron, your father would be proud of you.
MYRON *(proudly)*. Shuddap, Ma!

(Music swells as the lights dim, and the curtain falls.)

THE PLAY ENDS

NOTES

NOTES